CAE
Practice
Tests ▶ Plus

Alan Stanton
Susan Morris

Longman

Pearson Education Limited
Edinburgh Gate
Harlow
Essex CM20 2JE
England
and Associated Companies throughout the world

www.longman-elt.com

ISBN 0 582 36570 8

Set in 10.5pt Frutiger Light

Printed in Spain by Graficas Estella

Fourth impression 2000

Acknowledgements

We are grateful to the following for permission to reproduce
copyright photographs:

John Birdsall for 143 bottom; Sarah Boait for 135 bottom right;
Bristock-IFA for 129 bottom left (Bernd Ducke), 132 bottom (Bernd
Ducke), 134 middle left (Esbin Anderson) 134 bottom right
(Mountain Stock) and 138 middle right (Eric Bach); Camera Press /
Benoit Gysemberg for 136 top left; J Allan Cash for 136 bottom
right; Collections / Brian Schuel for 133 top left and 135 top left;
Collections / Geoff Howard for 131 bottom; Firepix International /
Tony Myers for 130 bottom; Robert Harding Picture Library /
D Maxell for 130 top; Robert Harding / Rolf Richardson for 131
middle right; Robert Harding Syndication / IPC Magazines for 135
bottom right; Image Bank / Don Klumpp for 138 top right; Kobal
Collection for 137 bottom left; © Pearson Education / Gareth Boden
for 141 bottom; © Pearson Education / Trevor Clifford for 140;
Photographers Library for 131 top left, 131 top right, 133 top right,
134 bottom left and 136 bottom left; Pictor International for 133
bottom, 143 top left, 143 top right and 143 middle right; Pictures
Colour Library for 139 bottom left; Rex Features for 132 top left;
Science Photo Library for 137 top middle (Celestial Image Co.), 137
top right (David Ducros), 137 top left and 137 bottom left (NASA);
Frank Spooner Pictures / Gamma for 142 top and 142 bottom; The
Stock Market for 129 bottom right, 136 top right and 139 top right
(Ned Gillette); Tony Stone Images for 129 top (Bruce Ayres), 131
middle left (Don Smetzer), 134 top left (Mark Romine), 134 top
right (Donovan Reese), 138 bottom (Christopher Bissell), 139 right
(Gavin Hellier) and 139 middle left (Robert Frerck); Telegraph Colour
Library for 132 top right (FPG / A Tilley), 135 top right (T Leighton),
138 middle left (FPG / R Chapple), 138 top left (Silvestris), 139 top
left (VCL), and 143 middle left (VCL)

We are grateful to the following for permission to reproduce
copyright material:

Andromeda Oxford Ltd for extracts from 'Insincerity' in EYE TO EYE
by Peter Marsh; BBC Wildlife Magazine for an extract from 'A Town
Like Davis' from BBC WILDLIFE Magazine 1990; Economist
Newspapers Ltd for an extract from 'Whales' in THE ECONOMIST
8.4.89 © The Economist, London 1989; Gruner & Jahr Ltd for
extracts from 'Why You Feel Under the Weather' in THE WORLD IN
FOCUS January 1993 and 'Aspects of Love: What is this thing called
love?' by Sharon Kingston & Amanda Cochrane in THE WORLD IN
FOCUS No 3 November 1993; Guardian Newspapers Ltd for extracts
from the articles 'History set in Stone' (adapted) in THE GUARDIAN
23.3.91, 'You must remember this' by Ian Hunt in THE GUARDIAN
9.1.93, 'Fast Forward' by Geoff Mulgan & Helen Wilkinson in THE
GUARDIAN 6.6.95, 'Simply the best' by Penny Cottee and 'The
Power of the spoken word' by Brian Keaney in THE GUARDIAN
27.4.97, 'Rites of Passage' by Nancy Rawlinson in THE GUARDIAN
17.6.97, 'They think it's all over' by John Duncan in THE GUARDIAN
8.1.98, 'The Writing on the Wall' by Oliver Swanton in THE
GUARDIAN 1.9.98, 'Across the gap' in THE GUARDIAN
(EDUCATION) 29.9.92, 'Safety Drive' by Peter Loxley in THE
GUARDIAN (EDUCATION) 19.1.93, 'A Telephone pioneer: Henry
Hunnings (1843–86)' by Mary Burgess in THE GUARDIAN
(EDUCATION) 27.4.93, 'Out of this World' by Mary Burgess in THE
GUARDIAN WEEKEND 14.11.92; 'Best of Times, Worst of Times' by
Rosanna Greenstreet in THE OBSERVER MAGAZINE 27.12.92; the
Controller of Her Majesty's Stationery Office for an extract from
'Shoplifting' in PRACTICAL WAYS TO CRACK CRIME published by
The Home Office, Crown Copyright; Independent Newspapers (UK)
Ltd for extracts from the articles 'A World without light, colour or
shape' by Tom Maley in THE INDEPENDENT 16.7.90, 'Terrorised by a
collar stud: the Worst of Times' by Glen Baxter in
THE INDEPENDENT 28.1.91, 'An English family, 80 years of
schooling' by Sarah Strickland in THE INDEPENDENT 28.5.92 and
'They said I was useless but look at me now' by Anne Nicholls in
THE INDEPENDENT 7.1.93; the author for an extract from 'Desert
discoveries and monster myths' by David Keys in THE INDEPENDENT
ON SUNDAY 2.12.90; the author Derek Parker for an extract from
his article 'Still Sprinting' in THE AUTHOR Spring 1990; Phaidon
Press Ltd for an extract from CHESS: AN ILLUSTRATED HISTORY by
Raymond Keene; Reader's Digest Association for extracts from 'The
Pull of the Land' in FACTS AND FALLACIES © Reader's Digest 1988,
'Are Women more romantic than men?', 'Going it alone', 'Why do
people sometimes fail to help when they should?' in MARVELS AND
MYSTERIES OF THE HUMAN MIND © The Reader's Digest 1992 and
'Staying healthy in Space' in READERS DIGEST 'How is it Done?'
column © The Reader's Digest 1990; the author for an extract from
'Springing hot from the bowels of the Earth' by June Sampson in
THE EUROPEAN 14–17 January 1993; Times Newspapers Ltd for
extracts from the articles 'That sweet smell of success' by Mark
Skipworth in THE SUNDAY TIMES 11.4.93 © Times Newspapers Ltd
1993, 'A consuming addiction' by Chris Johnston in THE TIMES
2.1.98 © Times Newspapers Ltd 1998; Peters Fraser & Dunlop
Group Ltd on behalf of the author, for an extract from 'Writers do it
lying down' by Joanna Trollope in GOOD HOUSEKEEPING February
1993.

We have been unable to trace the copyright holders of the articles
'Volcanoes: Dangers and Benefits' in BBC WORLD magazine,
November 1992, 'Sleep Easy' by Nadine Baggott, 'Story of your life'
by Jessica Bondy, 'Hello, hello operator' by Tom Quinn 'Heroes and
Villains – William Carlos Williams' by David Widgery, and would
appreciate any information which would enable us to do so.
Sample OMR sheets are reproduced by permission of the University
of Cambridge Local Examinations Syndicate.

Designed by Michael Harris
Project managed by Jayne Wildman

Contents

Exam Overview

The **Certificate in Advanced English** is a post-First Certificate exam which is offered three times a year, in March, June and December. There are five papers in the exam and each paper receives an equal weighting of 20 per cent of the marks. Papers are:

Paper 1	Reading	1 hour 15 minutes
Paper 2	Writing	2 hours
Paper 3	English in Use	1 hour 30 minutes
Paper 4	Listening	45 minutes (approximately)
Paper 5	Speaking	15 minutes (approximately)

CAE offers a high-level qualification to people wanting to use English for professional or study purposes and is much more advanced than FCE.

- The examination questions are task-based and simulate real-life tasks.

- Questions in Papers 1–3 are text-based. This means that there is always something to read before the task can be done.

- Rubrics in CAE are longer than in FCE or CPE. They need to be read carefully as they provide contexts for the questions.

- For Papers 1, 3 and 4 you will have to transfer your answers on to an answer sheet.

Paper	Formats	Test focus
Reading four texts, approximately 50 questions	**Parts 1 and 4:** multiple matching **Part 2:** gapped text **Part 3:** multiple choice	**Parts 1 and 4:** reading for the main ideas and specific information **Part 2:** text structure **Part 3:** detailed understanding of a text
Writing **Part 1:** one or two compulsory tasks **Part 2:** one task from a choice of four	**Parts 1 and 2:** from the following: formal and informal letters, articles, reports, reviews, memos, information leaflets, brochures, notices, competition entries, personal notes, instructions, directions and announcements	**Part 1 :** applying information from reading input, selecting, summarising and comparing to produce the writing task specified **Parts 1 and 2:** writing for a specific target reader, using appropriate layout, style and register
English in Use six texts, 80 questions	**Part 1:** 4-option multiple-choice cloze **Part 2:** open cloze **Part 3:** error correction **Part 4:** word formation **Part 5:** register transfer (completing a text using information from an input text) **Part 6:** discourse cloze (choosing sentences or phrases to complete a text)	**Part 1:** understanding lexis **Part 2:** understanding grammatical patterns **Part 3:** identifying extra wrong words or spelling / punctuation errors **Part 4:** word building from prompts **Part 5:** understanding and changing style and register **Part 6:** recognising coherence and cohesion
Listening four parts, 30–40 questions	**Parts 1 and 2:** informational monologue (Part 2 is heard once only); sentence completion or note-taking **Part 3:** dialogue with 2/3 speakers; multiple-choice, sentence completion, completing notes, matching ideas with speakers **Part 4:** five short extracts by five speakers; multiple-matching or 3-option multiple-choice	**Parts 1 and 2:** understanding the text as a whole and also detailed information **Part 3:** understanding specific information, opinions and attitudes **Part 4:** identifying speakers, topic, context, function, opinion and specific information
Speaking four parts	**Part 1:** exchange of information between two candidates and one examiner **Part 2:** each candidate speaks for one minute and makes a twenty-second comment after the other candidate has spoken **Part 3:** both candidates discuss a problem-solving task based on visual prompts while the examiner listens **Part 4:** both candidates continue the Part 3 discussion with the examiner	**Part 1:** general social and interactional language **Part 2:** describing and commenting on visual prompts and speaking at length **Part 3:** negotiating and collaborating **Part 4:** summarising, reporting, developing ideas from Part 3

PAPER 1 contains four texts of between 450 and 1,200 words each (a total of about 3,000 words), and about 45–50 reading comprehension questions. A text may be continuous, or consist of several short texts on a related topic. Texts are taken from the following sources: newspapers, magazines, journals, non-fiction books, brochures or leaflets. They can be informational, descriptive, narrative, persuasive, give advice or opinions, etc. You must transfer your answers to an answer sheet (see page 123).

Parts 1 and 4: Multiple Matching
(Part 1, pages 6–7; Part 4, pages 12–14)

For the multiple matching task, you have to match questions or statements with relevant information from the text, presented in the form of a list. Part 4 has a longer text than Part 1 and has more questions. It may consist of different texts on the same theme. This task tests your ability to find specific information in a text, including opinion or attitude, quickly and accurately.

Exam tips
- Read the instructions carefully. They contain information about the type of text (e.g. newspaper article) and what you have to read for (e.g. to match a list of opinions with the people who hold them).
- Skim the whole text quickly before you scan for the specific information required. This will give you an idea of what it is about and how it is organised.
- Underline key words and phrases in the questions and scan for parts of the text which contain the same ideas. They will probably be expressed in a different way from the question.
- Read carefully only those parts of the text where the answer is likely to be found. Don't waste time reading the whole text in detail.

Part 2: Gapped Text (pages 8–9)

This text has six or seven gaps with seven or eight extracts below the text. You have to choose the correct extract for each gap. One extract does not fit at all.

This task tests your ability to understand the structure and progression of a text, to identify a logical sequence of ideas and to understand linking words and discourse features.

Exam tips
- Read the main text first, ignoring the gaps. This will give you an idea of the subject matter and how it is organised.

- Highlight words that refer to people or places.
- Highlight time references – this will help you follow the sequence of events.
- Highlight linking words – this will help you follow the argument.
- Look for lexical and grammatical links between the main text and the paragraphs that have been removed.
- Look for links both before and after the gaps and at the beginning and end of the paragraphs.
- Check that the article makes sense when you read it as a complete text.

Part 3: Multiple Choice Questions
(pages 10–11)

There are five to seven questions on a text followed by four possible answers (A, B, C, D). You have to choose the correct answer. The questions usually follow the order of the text.

This task tests your ability to find specific information in the text, to deduce meaning from context and to understand small but important differences in meaning.

Exam tips
- Skim the text to get an idea of what it is about.
- Look at the questions first but not the four options.
- Find the section of the text that relates to each question.
- Underline key words in the questions and options.
- Highlight words in the text that confirm the answer. Correct answers will paraphrase facts and ideas in the text.
- Consider why the other answers are wrong – you can get the right answer by a process of elimination.

How is the Reading Paper marked?

One mark is given for each correct answer to the multiple matching tasks. Two marks are given for each correct answer to the multiple choice and gapped text tasks.

Paper 1 is objectively marked by an Optical Mark Reader (OMR), a computer system which is able to detect marks on paper. You indicate your answers on an answer sheet using a pencil, and this sheet is read by the OMR. You do not lose marks for incorrect answers.

Examples of OMR answer sheets for Papers 1, 3 and 4 are given on pages 123 to 126. You may use photocopies of these sheets to practise recording answers for each of the Practice Tests.

PAPER 1   Reading (1 hour 15 minutes)

PART 1

Answer questions **1–12** by referring to the newspaper article about university students and the jobs they have chosen on page **7**.

Indicate your answers **on the separate answer sheet**.

Tip Strip

Remember to:

• skim read the text quickly.

• underline key words and phrases in the questions.

• highlight names in the text. This will help you locate information more quickly.

Question 2: What type of job is Matthew looking for? How would you describe the job he has now? (paragraph 3)

Question 3: Kelly, Mike and Rebecca all mention financial difficulties. What was the result in each case?

Question 7: Which person works for him / herself? (paragraph 5)

Question 8: What does 'daunting' mean? (paragraph 1) Compare 'daunted' in paragraph 8.

For questions **1–12**, answer by matching the opinions expressed with the people listed (**A–E**) on the right below.

Some of the choices may be required more than once.

Note: When more than one answer is required, these may be given **in any order**.

Which person

stopped work after a short time?	**1**	
has a full-time temporary job?	**2**	
had to do something unwillingly because of a poor financial situation?	**3**	
misses friends on the course?	**4** **5**	**A** Matthew Bashford
has not left university yet?	**6**	**B** Mike Hale
finds an alternative to a job with a salary?	**7**	**C** Pete Fulford
feels confident about finding a job?	**8**	**D** Kelly Moore
found it difficult to get on with colleagues?	**9**	**E** Rebecca Jones
is not very ambitious with regard to future jobs?	**10**	
found a job easily?	**11**	
learnt a lot from a job?	**12**	

Rites of passage

Welcome to the world of work! How do students make the transition from campus to career?

THERE are aspects of student life that most graduates will happily leave behind; not many will miss writing essays at two in the morning, or cramming for exams. But for some students the only thing more daunting than doing a degree is finishing one. "Students have it easy" – it's one of those irritating things that people say. It's even more irritating when they turn out to be right.

Giving up student status means renouncing the laid-back lifestyle and three-month summer holidays. Instead, there is a soul-destroying search for work to look forward to. So are this year's graduates ready for the transition?

Matthew Bashford graduated a year ago from the University of Humberside with a degree in Business Studies. "It's awful," he says. "It makes you want to go back and be a student again. You find it difficult to get work in the first place, and when you do, it's menial stuff and the office politics are a nightmare – it's not easy to make friends." On top of that, full-time employment has not brought the deluge of cash Matthew expected. "After the increase in rent, bills, and income tax, I was better off as a student than I am now in terms of disposable income," he says. He is still seeking a permanent position.

For others, it is not only finding the job that is a problem, but also accepting the responsibility that goes with it. Mike Hale left Hertfordshire University with a law and economics degree. Lack of money meant he was forced back home which felt "like a regression", and he found it hard to adjust to the nine-to-five routine. "The thing is," he says, "college is so free and easy that even the thought of doing 40 hours a week is a bit intimidating. But you can't fight it, you've got to earn money. You have to become part of the system."

After working for nine months as a guitar technician, Mike had saved enough money to go travelling, an increasingly common choice for college leavers. But those who take the backpacking route have to start at the bottom of the career ladder when they return. Mike solved this problem by starting his own business.

Another common problem is that leaving university means losing the structure that a degree course provides. Pete Fulford, who left Coventry University with a BSc in industrial project design two years ago, says, "I got a bit depressed because there was a lot of camaraderie on my course, we were a very close-knit group. There was this institution that I was a part of, and then it was gone. It left a kind of void."

A year after leaving Brighton with a degree in design history, Kelly Moore was going through similar emotions. She said, "Going to lectures, being part of the system, it gives you a sense of security, and you lose that when you leave."

Not all students are daunted by the rite of passage from university to the jobs market. Rebecca Jones, a student of French and German from Liverpool University, is looking forward to leaving college and earning some money. She will take "any job going" to pay off her debts, although long-term career plans are vague. She mentions returning to France, where she spent part of her degree, and that she would be disappointed if she didn't use her language skills. "You don't know what it's going to be like until you get there, do you?"

Maybe not, but it is possible to plan. Those who have coped best are those who have thought about the difficulties they might face and are open to the diverse range of opportunities that may arise.

"I knew it was going to be hard," says Kelly, "but I had a game plan. I wanted to get a job that would help me pay off my debts, and I started applying as soon as I finished my course. I was offered a job as a personnel manager on the day I graduated. It certainly wasn't my ideal position, but it was an absolutely brilliant experience. It taught me self-discipline, how to organise myself and a great deal about the workplace. My advice is, don't just hope that something will come along, start planning what you're going to do as early as possible. It makes it so much easier."

For questions **13–18**, you must choose which of paragraphs **A–G** on page **9** fit into the numbered gaps in the following newspaper article. There is one extra paragraph which does not fit in any of the gaps.

Indicate your answers **on the separate answer sheet**.

A CONSUMING ADDICTION

Shopping used to be nothing more than a way of obtaining food, clothing and other necessities of life. Today, however, shopping symbolises the materialistic culture of western society and its popularity as a leisure activity reflects the rise of consumerism.

13

Having more money has meant spending patterns have changed. While traditional models of economic behaviour assume that consumers are rational and weigh up the costs and benefits before making a purchase, anyone who has ever walked into a shop and left five minutes later with a new jacket and £80 less in their wallet knows that this theory does not always hold true.

14

Her research on consumer behaviour identified impulsive buying as an attempt by shoppers to bolster their self-image, particularly for those who suffered from so-called compulsive buying or shopping addiction, a condition that affects 2 to 5 per cent of adults in the West.

The three-year study compared excessive buyers to a similar group of ordinary consumers. Excessive shoppers were more materialistic and believed that buying goods was a pathway to success, happiness and identity. "Excessive buying is a coping strategy to fill the gaps between how shoppers feel about themselves and the person they want to be," Dr Dittmar said.

15

Her research also reveals that certain types of goods are more likely to be bought on impulse than others. Those most frequently reported – clothes, jewellery, ornaments – are closely related to self-image and appearance. This finding is contrary to usual theories about impulse shopping, which explain it as a short-term gratification winning out over longer-term concerns such as debt.

16

In other words, shoppers were more willing to wait for "low impulse" goods such as kitchenware, than they were for clothes or other "high impulse" items. However, it was found that some of the 60 consumers asked to maintain a shopping diary for the study often regretted their impulsive purchases. Dr Dittmar said, "When people had explicitly bought for self-image reasons, regret was more likely to occur."

17

The conclusions drawn by Dr Dittmar about the treatment of compulsive shoppers are that prescribing anti-depressant drugs might solve the problem but only as long as sufferers continue to take them. Instead, they needed therapeutic help to address the underlying causes such as poor self-image.

18

"In no sense do *these people* directly force anyone to buy anything. But they are very sophisticated, making advertisements and shopping environments very seductive and playing on the idea that if you buy product X you will be much more attractive."

A Dr Dittmar said that the idea that consumers' impulsiveness differed, depending on the type of goods, was also supported by the finding that shoppers were less willing to delay gratification for items bought on impulse.

B But there are pitfalls, such as debt and addiction to buying. Addicts shop for shopping's sake rather than to buy what they need.

C Helga Dittmar, senior lecturer in psychology at Sussex University, has found that consumer goods are the material symbols of who a person is and who they would like to be.

D Her research also raises questions over the methods used to attract shoppers and encourage them to buy. Although advertisers and retailers increasingly appeal to consumers' self-image, Dr Dittmar said it was very difficult to argue that these factors were responsible for compulsive shopping.

E Although there were other ways of dealing with poor self-image, such as over-exercising or alcoholism, she said that shopping had become one of the most important strategies. This was especially true for women, who were three times more likely to be compulsive shoppers than men, as shopping was a socially approved activity, and allowed those who do not go out to work to get out of the house, Dr Dittmar said.

F But this finding was ambiguous because shopping addicts were more motivated by self-image than ordinary shoppers and were more likely to regret their actions. "It's not quite clear which way round this relationship goes, but there is a link between being very concerned with self-image goods and regretting impulse buying."

G This has been made possible by the 75 per cent increase in disposable income in the past 20 years. The number of credit cards in use has more than quadrupled, and the amount of outstanding consumer debt has almost tripled in the same period.

Read the following newspaper article and answer questions **19–24** on page **11**. On your answer sheet, indicate the letter **A**, **B**, **C** or **D** against the number of each question **19–24**. Give only one answer to each question.

Indicate your answers **on the separate answer sheet**.

HEROES AND VILLAINS

WILLIAM CARLOS WILLIAMS

BY DAVID WIDGERY

The first thing any practising doctor who also writes gets asked is, 'How do you find the time?' A combined career ought, in theory, to be perfectly possible: writers and doctors are both only trained observers. And there is a distinguished list of literary medics. But almost all end up doing one or the other. And if they are any good as writers, the stethoscope takes second place. There never seems to be time to do both properly.

But William Carlos Williams, the great Modernist poet, succeeded. Williams, who was born in 1883 and died in 1963 after a series of strokes, was not only a prolific poet, critic, novelist and dramatist, but also a life-long, full-time general practitioner in Rutherford, New Jersey. Although he could have easily set up a private practice in Manhattan, he chose instead to work in a working class industrial township with many recent immigrants from Italy and Eastern Europe, who spoke little English.

His 'Doctor Stories' deal with crises understood by any contemporary inner-city GP: still birth, autopsy, patients who refuse examination or cannot understand reassurance, never-ending family consultations in broken English, the particular test of night-visiting. My visits are made to the concrete tower-blocks of Tower Hamlets in London's East End, and the new immigrants are from Vietnam and Bangladesh.

There is no other writer who deals with how to listen, how to care, how to be there at the moment of physical need. He must have jotted these feelings down on prescription pad or notebook, then transcribed them on his laboratory typewriter, when hammering often awoke his children. 'By the time we assembled for breakfast, he had probably already done an hour's stint,' recalls his physician son William.

As much as his industry, I like his laconic tone. His tenderness is hard-edged, his humanism slightly cynical; best of all, he is never sentimental about the oppressed. And there is the sheer quality of his literary work.

Williams, whose mother was Puerto Rican, was only a second-generation English speaker, so he struggled to develop a truly American voice. His innovations were a simple way of writing with no similes and metaphors, using a syntax and rhythm based on lung breaths. It produced a wonderful, still woefully underrated body of work, ranging from the long love-poem 'Asphodel', to the haiku-like lilts in 'Pictures from Breugel'.

Williams is heroic because he was a prophet in his own land, because he reclaimed poetry from European-imitation academics and because he stayed a working doctor – and enjoyed it. 'I never felt', he wrote, 'that medicine interfered with me but rather that it was my food and drink, the very thing that made it possible to write.' So whenever I become disgruntled about the workload, I mutter a phrase of Williams's about one of his patients, which sums up my own mixed feelings about practising in the East End: 'her smile, with a shrug, always won me.'

19 How is William Carlos Williams unlike other literary doctors, according to David Widgery?

  A He enjoyed working as a doctor.
  B His work as a doctor was a source of ideas for his writing.
  C He managed to continue both careers for all his life.
  D His powers of observation developed with his writing.

20 The problems that Williams encountered among his patients

  A were typical of the time.
  B exist in similar settings today.
  C have disappeared with advances in medicine.
  D were specific to the region where he worked.

21 In which area is there a similarity between William Carlos Williams and David Widgery?

  A literary tastes
  B temperament
  C family origins
  D working environment

22 When did William Carlos Williams do his literary work?

  A at night
  B after evening surgery
  C during the afternoon
  D in the early morning

23 According to David Widgery, the reputation of William Carlos Williams

  A is now higher than it has ever been.
  B is not as high as it deserves to be.
  C has declined since his death.
  D has been overshadowed by that of his contemporaries.

24 Regarding his own medical work, David Widgery

  A fails to find it challenging.
  B sometimes wishes he had less to do.
  C continues practising for the sake of his patients.
  D finds it interferes with his aims as a writer.

Tip Strip

Remember:
- skim read the text for general understanding. Don't worry if you don't understand every word. Questions require you to interpret specific parts of the text, and not individual words.
- look at the questions, but not the four options before reading the text in more detail.
- find the section of the text that relates to each question.
- underline key words in the questions and options.

Question 19: Are all the options true? What is the key word in the question?

Question 22: Is there a time mentioned in the fourth paragraph?

Question 23: What does 'woefully underrated' mean in paragraph 6? Is the meaning positive or negative?

Tip Strip

Texts in Part 4 may be divided into sections. One approach to this task is to:

- read through the first section of the text only, then read through all the questions, matching the questions that refer to that section.
- do the same with the other sections, gradually reducing the number of questions you have to consider.

Question 30: Arithmetic involves adding up and subtracting numbers. Who mentions this?

Question 33: What was Elizabeth Brett unable to do and why?

Question 38: Who received a reference from a school? What kind of A level results did they get?

Answer questions **25–42** by referring to the information members of the Brett family give about their education on pages **13–14**.

Indicate your answers **on the separate answer sheet**.

For questions **25–42** choose your answers from the list of family members (**A–D**).

Some choices may be required more than once.

Which family member

says fellow-pupils expected to find jobs near where they lived?	25 ....
had potential that was not realised early?	26 ....
regrets the lack of career choice?	27 ....
suffered from hostility from people of the same age?	28 ....
had an education that did not continue to secondary level?	29 ....
did mental arithmetic?	30 ....
passed an examination to go on to secondary education?	31 ....
had parents who suffered financially to support his / her education?	32 ....
was prevented by the school from doing the desired choice of subjects?	33 ....
changed schools during secondary education?	34 ....
had teachers who treated boys and girls in the same way?	35 ....
recognised the benefits of a different learning approach?	36 ....
had to study with the constant fear of expulsion?	37 ....
exceeded the school's expectations?	38 ....
used technology to communicate with pupils in another country?	39 ....
failed an important exam?	40 ....
had decided on a profession before leaving school?	41 ....
was forced to study a favourite subject outside school?	42 ....

A Freda

B Brian

C Mike

D Elizabeth

An English Family, 80 Years of Schooling

Freda Brett, 85

I started school when I was four. I didn't learn anything at my first school, we just played. Then we moved and I went to a school a mile from home – I used to walk with my brother, the roads were safe then. The headmaster really was a cruel man, he used to beat the boys. I was about eight when we moved again and I went to another school where I was very happy. I don't think we learnt all that much – we did reading, writing, arithmetic, history and geography. The boys did gardening and the girls did needlework and housewifery. The whole school was in one room, divided into classes. We sat in rows of wooden desks facing the teacher who would write on the board and ask questions. We learnt to add up in our heads – they can't do that now. We never got any homework. We had singing lessons but no piano. There were nature lessons but no art lessons. Only two people went on to secondary education in my time. We had no ambition, but our parents never put us forward either. I suppose it was as much as they could do to support us. I wish we had the opportunity to have done more – there were not the chances there are now. We never had any special training for anything specific at school.

Brian Brett, 65

Discipline was enforced by fear at my first school. The headmaster was very brutal. The teachers tended to be elderly spinsters. Most learning was by rote. There wasn't a great deal of individual attention, and no homework. School was very much divorced from your home and parents.

We were a very poor family. It was a grind just to stay alive. You had no expectations really. Everyone worked locally. Each year the top class was entered for the county scholarship exam for grammar school in Stowmarket. Only one place each year went to someone from my school, and I got it. My parents had to make a great financial sacrifice to send me there. My fees were paid for, but I needed things like a uniform which cost two or three weeks' worth of my father's wages. I got a free bus pass and was entitled to free school meals too, but that was looked upon by my parents as charity, so I

took sandwiches. If I hadn't got the scholarship, I would have gone to the area school and left at about 14. Instead, my parents signed a piece of paper saying I would stay until I was 16. They were aware it might lead to something better. It tended to mean you went from blue collar to white collar. I was an outcast among my own kind: virtually ostracised. It was very difficult, not being part of the troop that roamed the village.

We did English grammar and literature, chemistry, botany and religious education. French was compulsory. The girls did cookery and prepared school meals, the boys did woodwork. There were no visual aids. There was much greater discipline because there was always the threat of being expelled. It was a very narrow education.

Mike Brett, 42

I went to four different primary schools. I quite liked school, although I didn't know what was going on. My last year was spent in a middle-class urban school that was much more formal. There was a lot of rote-learning, and I was introduced to some subjects for the first time, such as classics. It was obvious that the 11-plus examination figured prominently in the school's thoughts. I think it was a shock to my parents, because it was also obvious that I wasn't going to pass it. They got me a private tutor, but I failed anyway. My father was very disappointed. All my friends bar one passed the 11-plus; that still hurts today. It was totally iniquitous. I felt a failure for years after that. Education for me was a dawning process: I was a late developer. My mother told me recently that when one teacher wrote: 'He will never achieve anything in life' in my report, I was determined to prove him wrong.

So I went to the secondary modern. Discipline was rigorously enforced. Some of the teachers were absolutely brutal. It was part of the culture of the institution. It was expected that everyone in my class would do O level examinations. I scraped five. My father was amazed. I was surprised, to be honest. I remember my parents visiting the school. There had been some discussion at home about my progress. I had another private tutor for a few years, so they were obviously interested and concerned. They thought of education as a positive force in life, a passport. My mother in particular wanted me to have the opportunities she hadn't had. And by then I knew I wanted to teach.

We moved, and I applied for a place at Felixstowe Grammar School. The head wasn't too keen to take me, but I got in to do history, geography and economics A levels. One of my economics teachers was quite different from other teachers I'd had. He asked us to read things and discuss them. I found it much easier to learn that way. I even remember having a lesson on a fishing boat. But the other subjects were still taught formally from the teacher's notes, a very prescriptive approach.

The school wouldn't support my going to university. I was pointed towards teacher training. But then the A level examination results came out, the school changed its mind and gave me a reference, so I went to Lancaster University to read history and economics.

Elizabeth Brett, 14

Mum taught me to read before I went to school. I remember waiting for Dad to come home so that I could read to him; I used to love it. At school you had reading cards to take home. You had to read three more pages of your book to your parents, then they had to sign a card to say you'd done it. I loved primary school. The thing I enjoyed the most was the music. I played the recorder in school concerts and started to learn the violin. We had penpals in Tasmania who we communicated with by computer. There was lots of painting. Most of my teachers made particular emphasis that boys and girls are equal: if one of the children made a sexist comment, the teacher always made sure they were stopped.

My present school is very big. You don't feel like an individual really. I had to decide on my GCSE examination options last month – it was really hard. I couldn't do what I wanted to do – music and two languages. They wouldn't let me, they insisted I took a course like home economics, child development or business. I could see the point but felt it was putting me behind in what I wanted to do. I'm having to do an extra evening class in music which means more work.

I don't know what I'd like to do afterwards – something to do with music. I want to go to university definitely. I'm proud of what my parents have done and I don't think they'd have got this far if they hadn't gone to university. I don't just want to leave school and get a job. I don't think I'd be ready to face the world. ■

Guide to PAPER 2   Writing

PAPER 2 consists of two parts and you will have to answer two questions in total. Questions specify the type of writing required (e.g. letter, report, article or leaflet) and the target audience (e.g. company, colleague, friend or magazine readers).

Part 1   (pages 16–17)

In this part there is a compulsory question to answer. You will have to read up to 450 words of input, such as a letter or advertisement, before you start writing. Sometimes there are 'handwritten' notes on the input material which you must also take into account.

Part 2   (page 18)

In this part there are four questions and you must do one of them. Each question is described in about 4–5 lines. There will always be one work-related question.

For each answer you should write about 250 words.

Exam tips

- You do not have to answer the first question first. You can start with any question.
- Make sure you know the lay-out for:
  - formal letters
  - informal letters
  - memos, reports
  - newspaper magazine articles
  - brochures, leaflets
- For Part 1 include all the relevant information from the input. Avoid using whole phrases from the texts. Use your own words.
- For Part 2, choose a topic you are familiar with.
- For each question, read the instructions carefully and highlight key words. These will tell you:
  - the type of writing required
  - the target audience
  - the points that must be included
- Decide on a suitable register for your target audience.
- Decide on the number of paragraphs before you start writing. Plan the content of each paragraph.
- Follow your plan and write your answer once. You may not have time to do a first draft and a second version.
- Allow time to check your work carefully. Make sure you have included all the points necessary and that your answer is about the right length.

How is the Writing Paper marked?

Each question is marked on a six-point scale of 0–5. There is a general impression mark-scheme that applies to all questions and refers to general features such as:

- task achievement or completion of a task with no omissions.
- use of an appropriate register.
- the effect on the target reader.
- clear and consistent organisation of material.
- natural and accurate use of language.
- use of a range of vocabulary and grammatical structures.
- use of a variety of cohesive devices.

There is also a task mark-scheme produced for each particular question outlining the points that must be mentioned.

Each paper is marked by two trained examiners, and the scores are added together to provide the total mark for this paper.

PART 1

1   You have recently been on holiday in the USA. During your holiday you were injured and had to pay for medical treatment. You made a claim on your travel insurance policy and have now received a letter from the insurance company.

Read the letter from the insurance company below with your handwritten notes on it, and your medical bill, the exchange rates given and the newspaper article on page 17. Then, **using the information carefully**, write a reply to the insurance company's letter explaining why you are not satisfied with their offer.

Write approximately 250 words. You should use your own words as far as possible. You do not need to include addresses.

Apex Insurance plc

1 Ledbury Square
Melchester
Wessex
MC1 2AN

30 May 20 - -

Why the delay?

Dear ....

Re: Claim for Medical Expenses

Thank you for your letter of 15 April concerning your claim for medical expenses incurred while on holiday in Florida, USA.

After giving careful consideration to your claim, it has been decided that it is not possible for us to pay your medical expenses in this case. Your claim cannot be met because it is excluded by the terms of the insurance policy which clearly state (Section 4.1 (a)):

'The company shall not be liable to meet medical expenses incurred as a result of wilful and reckless self-exposure to danger of the Person Insured.'

Can't possibly apply in my case.

However, as a gesture of goodwill, we are prepared to cover the cost of the new pair of shoes that you were obliged to purchase in Florida, and for which you sent us the receipt (for $100). We therefore enclose a cheque for £30.

We do hope that you have now fully recovered from the injuries.

This can't be right. What exchange rate did they use?

Yours sincerely

Fergus Wolff

Fergus Wolff
Chief Claims Negotiator

Green Heights Hospital

Fort Lauderdale,
Florida,
USA

Fracture of right wristbone
Two broken fingers
Lacerations

$5,000

A. Dodd

Paid 3 April, 20 – –

EXCHANGE RATES

Your dollar today is worth:

France — FF 6.0 (franc)
Germany — DM 1.78 (Mark)
Japan — ¥142 (yen)
UK — £0.6 (pound)

FORT LAUDERDALE POST

1 APRIL, 20 – –

Boy rescued from Alligator Pool

At Fort Lauderdale Zoo early yesterday morning a six-year-old local boy, Larry Delgado, was rescued in the nick of time from the snapping jaws of a dozen alligators. Larry had climbed the fence, just before feeding time, to get a better view, when he lost his balance and fell into the alligator pool. Immediately, a dozen hungry monsters advanced towards him. Luckily for Larry, a visitor to the zoo, believed to be a tourist from Europe, leapt over the fence and helped Larry to safety, while fending off the alligators with blows from a rolled-up newspaper and some well-aimed kicks at their noses. Larry was unhurt and soon reunited with his anxious parents, but our hero suffered a severe bite to the hand and was immediately taken to hospital in an ambulance. The alligators contented themselves with chewing up two black leather shoes and a copy of the London *Times*.

Tip Strip

Question 1: Think about your target audience. You will need to write a formal letter. Include:
- the name of the person you are writing to
- a suitable date for your letter (how long after the letter you have received?)
- a suitable formal ending (look at the ending in the input letter)

Remember, it's not necessary to include addresses.

- Take your main points from the annotations on the letter and plan your answer.
- Use the input texts to provide evidence to support your arguments. Summarise information in the newspaper report but express it in a neutral way. Avoid informal phrases such as 'hungry monsters' – use the word 'alligators' instead.
- Write at least three paragraphs. Be polite but at the same time express your dissatisfaction. Clearly state your demand (more compensation) in your final paragraph.

Tip Strip

Choose **one** of the following writing tasks. Your answer should follow exactly the instructions given. Write approximately 250 words.

Question 2

• You have to write an article for newspaper readers so use:
  – a headline.
  – sub-headings.
  – a fairly colloquial style.
• Write about two or three restaurants. Name them and say where they are.
• Add points of your own – the phrase 'and so on' encourages you to do this.
• Write an article which is complimentary.

Question 3

• This is a formal report so lay it out like this:

To: ...
From: ...
Subject: ...
Date: ...

• You can number the paragraphs and / or give them headings.
• Make sure you give examples of and suggest <u>solutions</u> for each problem.

Question 4

• Consider your target audience. Use an informal and fairly colloquial style.
• Write a headline and use sub-headings based on key words in the question, e.g.

The <u>pleasures</u> of ...
Possible <u>problems</u>
<u>Equipment</u> you will need
How much will it <u>cost</u>?

2 A local newspaper has invited readers to send in an article about two or three restaurants in the area which they think are worth eating at. The restaurants can be from any price range, but they must be worth recommending from a particular point of view, such as quality of cooking, pleasant setting, value for money and so on. The article will be published and the newspaper will pay for a meal for two at one of the restaurants described.

Choose the restaurants you would recommend and write the **article**.

3 The principal of the school (or college) where you are studying English has received many complaints from students that the building is untidy, is not cleaned properly and needs some repairs. The principal has asked you to write a report, describing the most serious problems and suggesting how things can be improved.

Write your **report** for the principal.

4 A student magazine is running a series of articles entitled 'Starting a New Hobby or Sport'. The editor has asked you to contribute an article to this series. Describe the pleasures and possible problems of your chosen hobby or sport. Mention any equipment that is needed and what costs are involved.

Write your **article** for the magazine.

5 You have seen the following job advertised and have decided to apply for the post.

Melchester Arts Festival Organising Committee

Administrative Assistant
Full-time Temporary (one-year) Post
Salary £25,000

We are looking for someone to undertake a wide range of administrative duties in connection with the Melchester Arts Festival which takes place in July and August every year. The successful candidate need not have previous experience of this type of work but must:

• speak English and at least one other language.
• have a pleasant telephone manner.
• be methodical and have an eye for detail.

Write your **letter of application**.

Question 5

• This is a formal letter (see Question 1). You will need about five paragraphs.
• Make sure you mention:
  – the job you are applying for and where you saw the advertisement.
  – your educational qualifications.
  – your previous experience.
  – evidence that you have the three abilities mentioned in the advertisement.
  – when you are available for interview.

Guide to PAPER 3
English in Use

PAPER 3 has six parts, and a total of 80 questions. For each part there is a short text on which the questions are based.

This paper tests your knowledge of vocabulary, grammar, spelling and punctuation, error correction, word formation, style and register, and coherence and cohesion in texts. You must transfer your answers to an answer sheet (see pages 124–125).

Part 1: Multiple Choice Cloze (page 21)

This is a text with 15 single-word gaps. For each gap, you choose your answer from four options: A, B, C or D.

This question is mainly a test of vocabulary, but may contain some grammatical words, such as linking words.

Exam tips
- Read through the text for meaning before reading the four options.
- The four words often have similar meanings but only one will collocate with the other words in the sentence. Look carefully at the words surrounding the gap.
- Fixed expressions and phrasal verbs may be tested in this type of question. You should learn phrases rather than just single words.
- Guess if necessary. You will not lose marks by choosing a wrong answer.
- When you have finished, read the text again to check that your answers make sense.

Part 2: Open Cloze (page 22)

This is a text with 15 single-word gaps. You have to complete the text with structural words such as: *has*, *been*, *the*, *so*, *which*, *in*. This question tests your knowledge of grammatical patterns.

Exam tips
- Read the text once straight through for general understanding.
- Identify the type of word missing in each gap.
- You know all the words – the problem is to think of them. Try thinking of all the auxiliary verbs, pronouns, relatives and prepositions that you know.
- The words *which* and *whose* always seem difficult to get. Bear these two words in mind when you can't fill a gap.

- Only write one word in each gap.
- Look carefully at the surrounding context of each gapped word. Check that your word makes sense.

Part 3: Error Correction (page 23)

The task will be either:

1 a text in which most lines have an extra wrong word. You have to identify the extra words. (page 23)

or:

2 a text which contains spelling and punctuation mistakes that you have to correct. (page 47)

This task tests either your knowledge of grammatical patterns and sentence structure or your knowledge of spelling and punctuation. Both task types test your ability to read with care and attention.

Exam tips
- Read through the whole text once for general understanding.
- Remember that most lines have a mistake. Only 3–5 lines are correct.
- Study the examples carefully because they give you valuable information about how to record your answers.

For tasks which test wrong words:
- You are looking for words that are wrong, not just unnecessary.
- The wrong words are usually short, for example, prepositions, articles, auxiliary verbs, conjunctions.
- You will need to read the whole sentence across several lines, not just one line, in order to find wrong words.
- A wrong word does not appear twice in the same line.

For tasks which test spelling and punctuation look for these types of errors:
- doubled final consonants.
- omission of silent letters.
- additional final *e*.
- incorrectly spelled prefixes and suffixes.
- commas, full stops and brackets which are either unnecessary or missing.
- small letters instead of capitals, or the other way round.
- apostrophes, either missing or unnecessary.
- hyphens, either missing or unnecessary.

Part 4: Word Formation (page 24)

This consists of two short texts with 15 gaps in total. For each gap, a base word (the prompt word) is given. You have to form the correct word for the gap using this prompt word.

Exam tips

- Read through the texts first to get an idea of what they are about.
- Decide what part of speech you need for each gap. The word you need could be a noun, verb, adjective or adverb.
- Look at the base word. You may need to:
  – add a prefix (at the beginning),
    e.g. *appear* > *disappear*
  – add a suffix (at the end),
    e.g. *disappear* > *disappearance*
  – change the middle,
    e.g. *strong* > *strength*
  ... or a combination of these.
- At least one word in each text will need a prefix.
- There may be more than one change to a word. A change usually involves making the word longer.
- Be careful about negatives and plurals. Make sure that the text makes sense as whole.

Part 5: Register Transfer (page 25)

This consists of two short texts in different styles. The second text has 13 gaps and must be completed using the information, but not the words, in the first text.

Exam tips

- Read through both texts first. Is the first part more formal or less formal than the second part, which you have to complete?
- In some questions, there may not be a very obvious difference in style between the two texts, but the texts will be of different types and directed to a different target reader.
- The first part contains all the information you need but not the words. Highlight the words and phrases that you have to re-express.
- Check the instruction for the number of words you can use – usually one or two in each gap.
- Check that the information in the gapped text is the same as in the first text.

Part 6: Discourse Cloze (page 26)

This part consists of a text with six clauses, phrases or short sentences missing. You have to identify the missing phrases or sentences by choosing from a list of ten options.

Exam tips

- Read the text quickly to get an idea of what it's about.
- Look carefully at words and phrases such as 'it', 'which', 'because', and 'on the other hand' and try to work out what they refer to. This will help you follow the sequence of ideas.
- Consider whether the writer is giving an example, making an additional point or pointing out a disadvantage. This will help you to choose an appropriate answer.
- In some texts, all the options will fit grammatically so pay attention to the meaning. You need to understand the text as a whole.
- When you have finished, read the completed text, checking grammar and punctuation carefully.

How is the English in Use Paper marked?

Paper 3 is marked by trained markers using a mark-scheme. There is one mark per answer and correct spelling is essential. Once the answer sheets have been marked, they can be read by an Optical Mark Reader (OMR).

PAPER 3   English in Use (1 hour 30 minutes)

PART 1

Tip Strip

Remember to:

• read through the text for meaning before looking at the four options.

• consider carefully the words surrounding each gap.

• check that your answers make sense.

Question 2: Which word is most closely associated with animals?

Question 4: The meaning is clearly negative. Which word emphasises this?

Question 11: Which verb collocates with 'to extinction'?

Question 13: Which word means a permanent change in the weather?

Question 15: Which word collocates with 'of sunlight'?

For questions **1–15**, read the text below and then decide which word best fits each space. Put the letter you choose for each question in the correct box on your answer sheet. The exercise begins with an example (**0**).

Example: | 0 | *A* | | 0 |

History Set in Stone

Many species of animals and plants have disappeared from the earth. They have died out, or become (**0**) .... . But sometimes animals or plant (**1**) *D*... can be found buried in rocks. These are called fossils. Imprints in rocks (**2**) (*B* prints, for example) are also called fossils.

Not every creature (**3**) *A*. as a fossil. Many simply rot away completely and leave no (**4**) *D*.. of their existence. Because many creatures and plants have disappeared without leaving any fossils, we will never know anything about them.

The study of fossils, or palaeontology, to give it its scientific (**5**) *A*.., became established at the beginning of the nineteenth century. Before this research began, people did not believe that fossils had once been (**6**) *C*. . Large fossil teeth were seen as evidence of a race of giants in the past, while ammonites, a very (**7**) *A*. type of fossil which you might easily find yourself on a beach or among rocks, were called snakestones because of their snake-like (**8**) *C*. . People believed that snakes had been (**9**) *D*... to stone by a miracle.

The most famous fossils of all are the dinosaurs. There are, of course, no dinosaurs on (**10**) *A*.. in zoos. They were not (**11**) *B*. to extinction by humans as some animals have been, but became extinct millions of years before our own species developed. The reason why the dinosaurs became extinct is still a mystery. Many theories have (**12**) *A*. the disappearance of dinosaurs with major (**13**) *D*... change.

One possibility is that a gigantic meteorite crashed into the earth (**14**) *D*. so much dust into the atmosphere that the (**15**) *D*.. of sunlight was reduced. The temperature would have fallen and, as a consequence, many types of plants and animals would have become extinct.

0	(A)	extinct	B	extinguished	C	remote	D	obsolete
1	A	bones	B	evidence	C	parts	D	remains ✓
2	A	toe	B	paw	C	palm	D	hand ✓
3	A	lasts	(B)	survives	C	continues	D	develops ✗
4	A	marks	B	proof	C	remnants	D	trace ✓
5	A	name	B	term	C	description	D	status ✓
6	(A)	alive	B	physical	C	living	D	flesh ✗
7	A	common	B	usual	C	normal	D	frequent ✓
8	A	type	B	manner	C	shape	D	figure ✓
9	A	petrified	B	made	C	ossified	D	turned ✓
10	A	exhibition	B	appearance	C	sight	(D)	display ✗
11	(A)	hunted	B	brought	C	chased	D	driven ✗
12	A	connected	B	joined	C	explained	D	initiated ✓
13	(A)	climatic	B	temporal	C	weather	D	seasonal ✗
14	A	disturbing	(B)	displacing	C	putting	D	pushing ✗
15	A	heat	(B)	amount	C	degree	D	period ✗

For questions **16–30** complete the following article by writing each missing word in the correct box on your answer sheet. **Use only one word for each space.** The exercise begins with an example (**0**).

Example: | 0 | *why* | 0 |

Language Variety

The fact that English has been spoken in England for 1,500 years but in Australia for only 200, explains (**0**) .... we have a great wealth of regional dialects in England that is more or less totally lacking in Australia. It is often possible to tell where an English person comes from to (**16**) .... about 15 miles or less. In Australia, where (**17**) .... has not been enough time for changes to bring about (**18**) .... regional variation, it is almost impossible to tell where someone comes from at (**19**) ...., although very small differences are now beginning to appear. It is unlikely, however that there will (**20**) .... be as much dialectal variation in Australia as there is in England. This is because modern transport and communication conditions are very different from (**21**) .... they were 1,500 or (**22**) .... 100 years ago. Even (**23**) .... English is now spoken in many different parts of the world many thousands of miles apart, it is very unlikely that English will ever break up into (**24**) .... number of different non-intelligible languages in the same way that Indo-European and Germanic (**25**) .... German and Norwegian became different languages because the ancestors of the speakers of these two languages moved apart geographically, and were no (**26**) .... in touch and communicating with one another. In the modern world, barring unforeseen catastrophes, (**27**) .... will not happen, at (**28**) .... in the near future. As long as Americans and British people, for instance, are in touch with one another and want to communicate with one another, it is most unlikely that their dialects (**29**) .... drift so far apart (**30**) .... to become different languages.

Tip Strip

Remember:

- only 3–5 lines are correct.
- you are looking for **wrong** words.
- you need to read the whole sentence to find the wrong words.
- incorrect words only occur **once** in a line.

Line 31: Is the phrasal verb correct?

Line 34: Is there a previous mention of 'insincere remarks and flattery'?

Line 37: Is this talent 'unique' to humans? See lines 31–32.

Line 40: There are three prepositions in this line. Are they all necessary?

Line 41: Do you need a reflexive verb here?

In **most** lines of the following text there is **one** unnecessary word. It is either grammatically incorrect or does not fit in with the sense of the text. For each numbered line **31–46**, find this word and then write it in the box on your answer sheet. Some lines are correct. Indicate those lines with a tick (✓). The exercise begins with two examples (**0**).

Examples:

0	*any*	0
00	✓	0

Insincerity

0	....	The ability to deceive any others is thought by some psychologists
00	....	to be a characteristic that has been genetically selected through
31	....	human evolution. Comparisons have been made up with animal
32	....	deception, such as the camouflage and mimicry. For hundreds of
33	....	those generations, it is argued, the ability to make others
34	....	believe such insincere remarks and promises has conferred
35	....	advantages in struggles to control resources and win mating
36	....	with partners. The less cunning have, quite simply, produced
37	....	fewer offspring, and a unique talent for creating false impressions
38	....	has dominated the human gene pool. Whatever the merits or
39	....	shortcomings of this line of sharp thinking, there are undoubtedly
40	....	many of occasions in everyday social encounters when people, for
41	....	one reason or another, want to avoid themselves expressing their
42	....	true feelings. The ability to do this varies and success tends to
43	....	breed success. Those who lie effectively will have tend to lie more
44	....	often, perfecting their social skills in the process. Those who fail
45	....	are deterred from some future attempts and get less practice. With
46	....	lying, as is with everything else, practice makes perfect.

Tip Strip

Remember:
- decide which part of speech you need for each gap.
- at least one word in each text will have a prefix.
- check that the text makes sense as a whole.

Question 48: Does 'enrolment' give you a clue?

Question 50: Is it singular or plural?

Question 53: Is this positive or negative?

Question 57: How many adjectives can you form from 'satisfy'?

Question 58: Be careful of the spelling of this word.

Question 61: Is this singular or plural?

For questions **47–61** read the two texts below. Use the words in the boxes to form **one** word that fits in the same numbered space in the text. Write the new word in the correct box on your answer sheet. The exercise begins with an example (**0**).

Example: | 0 | *description* | | **0** |

INFORMATION LEAFLET

Application details

A full job (**0**) .... will be sent to all those selected for interview, but before sending in your application for this post, please note that the Overseas Marketing Officer has (**47**) .... for:

* (**48**) .... and enrolment of overseas students.
* confirming students' suitability for courses. This includes checking educational qualifications.
* marketing specialist courses in technical and (**49**) .... training.
* giving presentations to staff and (**50**) .... of overseas organisations.
* providing advice and assistance that will (**51**) .... students to complete visa and immigration (**52**) .... satisfactorily.
* preparing leaflets, brochures and other informational material for distribution in overseas markets.

Interviews will be held on 30 July. If you have not heard from us by 20 July, you may assume that your application has been (**53**) .... on this occasion.

(**0**)	DESCRIBE
(**47**)	RESPONSIBLE
(**48**)	RECRUIT
(**49**)	COMMERCE
(**50**)	REPRESENT
(**51**)	ABLE
(**52**)	PROCEED
(**53**)	SUCCESS

ADVERTISEMENT

A job in the theatre

The Red Parrot Theatre Company is putting on a new production of Macbeth and is looking for an (**54**) .... person to take charge of (**55**) .... Since we are an amateur company we can't offer any (**56**) .... reward but if you are interested in the theatre, it is very (**57**) .... work. It's part-time, of course, because we only do about three plays (**58**) .... The job involves making (**59**) .... with printers and placing advertisements in newspapers and whatever else needs doing. All expenses, such as phone calls will be (**60**) .... and you get four free tickets for every (**61**) .... If you are interested, come along to our first rehearsal on 27 June for an informal discussion of what is involved.

(**54**)	ENERGY
(**55**)	PUBLIC
(**56**)	FINANCE
(**57**)	SATISFY
(**58**)	ANNUAL
(**59**)	ARRANGE
(**60**)	FUND
(**61**)	PERFORM

Tip Strip

Remember to:

• read through both texts first. Is the first part more formal or less formal than the second part?

• highlight information in the first text that you have to re-express.

Question 62: What is a more formal word for 'turned up'?

Question 65: The key phrase is 'all reps'. They all had the same opinion, so what was complete?

Question 66: The letter uses the colloquial phrase 'worse than useless' and the memo has the word 'not ...' . You need a positive word to go with it.

Question 68: 'Get through' in the sense of successfully telephone is the idea that you need to re-express. What were they unable to do?

Question 72: Representatives don't want to be 'kept in the dark'. Can you think of an adjective meaning 'not to know'?

For questions **62–74**, read the following informal note that you have received from a colleague and use the information to complete the numbered gaps in the memo. Then write the new words in the correct space on your answer sheet. **Use no more than two words** for each gap. The words you need **do not occur** in the note. The exercise begins with an example (**0**).

Example:

0	*All*		0
			☐ ▨

Dear Bob

Could you do me a favour and write a memo for me (to the MD) about yesterday's meeting? I've had to go to our Edinburgh office (an emergency!). Here are the details:

Everyone turned up. We started after lunch and finished at 4.30. All reps complained that their cars were too small to carry all the stuff they had to show the customers and also that their car-phones were worse than useless in most parts of the South-West. Also they couldn't get through to Head Office after six because everybody had gone home. They also wanted to know why nobody got back to them or even let them know when a customer complained – because they often called on a customer and found they were in the dark about a problem he or she was having. I said I'd look into things and see them again – but we didn't fix a date.

Ann

MEMO

Titan Agricultural Products PLC

To: Charles Knightly, Managing Director
From: Antoinette Desmolines
Date: 3 March 20 – –
Subject: Sales Representatives' Meeting, 2 March 20 – –

(**0**) .... the sales representatives from the South-West Region (**62**) .... the meeting, which commenced at 2 p.m. and finished at 4.30. The representatives expressed (**63**) .... with the cars the company had provided them with on the grounds that they were too small for the (**64**) .... that they were obliged to carry with them for customers to examine. There was complete (**65**) .... on this point. They also said that their car-phones were not (**66**) .... in large parts of the South West. Another (**67**) .... they made was that they were unable (**68**) .... Head Office in the (**69**) .... because it was (**70**) .... Another problem was that when a customer complained, no one from Head Office (**71**) .... of the situation. Often they would visit a customer and find that they were (**72**) .... of the situation. I promised (**73**) .... these matters and report back to them at (**74**) .... meeting.

Tip Strip

Remember to:

• look carefully at words and phrases such as 'because', 'also', 'which' and try to work out what they refer to.

• when you have finished, read the text carefully, checking grammar and punctuation.

Question 75: Use your knowledge of conditional sentences.

Question 76: The first part of the sentence says 'begin'. The second part should refer to a later time.

Question 77: Are scientists likely to find out or not?

Question 79: Is there a phrase that comments on the importance of exercise?

Question 80: Which word is the opposite of 'dream'?

For questions **75–80** read through the following text and then choose from the list **A–J** below the best phrase to fill each of the spaces. Write one letter (**A–J**) in the correct box on your answer sheet. **Some of the suggested answers do not fit at all.** The exercise begins with an example (**0**).

Example: | 0 | *J* | | 0 |

Staying Healthy in Space

The range of foods available to astronauts is vast, and great care is taken to ensure that it looks and smells appetising. Meals are organised to provide an average of 3,000 calories a day, (**0**) .... . But astronauts can expend a great deal of energy in doing the simplest things. For example, if they try to turn a handle, they turn themselves as well. If they bend down to do up a shoelace, (**75**) .... . Finding unusual ways of doing such ordinary things uses up the excess calories. The space diet is balanced rather differently from a terrestrial diet. This is to try and compensate for changes that take place in the body during space flight. Bodily changes begin as soon as astronauts go into space (**76**) .... . Among the most serious is calcium loss, which causes a marked reduction in the mass and strength of bones. There is also a progressive loss of red blood cells. What causes these effects is not known, (**77**) .... . The heart muscles, with no gravity to battle against, start to waste away. The leg muscles start to waste away too, since walking, as done on Earth, (**78**) .... . Exercise also helps to reduce muscle wastage (**79**) .... . No one yet knows the limit of human endurance in space. If astronauts can withstand two years or more of continuous weightlessness, then mankind's dream of visiting other planets (**80**) .... .

A   and the question must be answered before long-duration space-flight is really safe
B   and are quite noticeable after even a week
C   they start turning somersaults
D   and will never be known
E   which is rather more than astronauts really need
F   and is vital on very long flights
G   could become reality in the early decades of the next century
H   can only be done if astronauts put on their heavy spacesuits
I   but they do not seriously threaten the health of astronauts

J   which seems high for living in an enclosed environment in which there is no gravity

Guide to PAPER 4   Listening

PAPER 4 consists of four parts. Parts 1, 3 and 4 are heard twice, but Part 2 is heard once only. The spoken texts will resemble radio programmes, telephone messages, interviews, personal statements, conversations, talks and lectures, and real life situations.

This paper tests your understanding of the text as a whole, of detailed information, opinions and attitudes, and context and function. You must transfer your answers on to an answer sheet (see page 126).

Parts 1 and 2 (pages 28 and 29)

These are monologues with a high informational content. To answer these parts, you will have to complete sentences or notes on a table or grid.

Part 3 (page 30)

This has two or more speakers who will express various attitudes and opinions. To answer Part 3, you will either:

– have to complete sentences or notes.

or:

– choose from multiple choice options.

Part 4 (page 31)

This consists of five short extracts from five different speakers, all speaking on a similar theme. To answer Part 4, you will either:

– have to match the speakers to two sets of five (out of eight) topics, contexts, situations or contexts.

or:

– choose from ten three-option (**A**, **B**, **C**) multiple-choice questions.

How is the Listening Paper marked?

Paper 4 is marked by trained markers using a mark-scheme. There is one mark per answer and in some cases correct spelling may not be essential. Once the answer sheets have been marked, they can be read by an Optical Mark Reader (OMR).

Exam tips

- Use every opportunity to listen to English in as many different situations as possible – conversations, radio, television, lectures, announcements, etc. All these may feature in Paper 4.
- Listen to different accents. Paper 4 may feature British regional accents and non-British accents.
- Learn to listen not just to what people say, but to the way they say it.

Parts 1, 2 and 3

- Check whether you must answer with a letter, a number, a word or a short phrase. Paper 4 questions ask for answers in a variety of formats.
- Read the questions before you listen to try and predict the most likely answer.
- Incomplete sentences often paraphrase what is on the recording, so listen for different ways of saying the same thing.
- In sentence completion tasks, check that the word or phrase fits grammatically. Pay attention to whether you need to use a singular or a plural.
- For multiple-choice questions read the stems before listening, but not the options. When you listen for the first time note down the answers. Before the second listening read the options carefully and choose the best answer.

Part 4

- Before listening read the questions and think of words you expect to hear in connection with the topic.
- For the second task you may have to listen to the tone of voice and the attitude of the speaker.
- Take care when transferring your answers to the answer sheet. Keep them in the correct order.

PAPER 4

Listening (approx. 45 minutes)

You will hear a lecturer talking to students at the beginning of their course. For questions **1–10**, fill in the missing information.

You will hear the recording twice.

Course Information

Course name: _____ **1**

People not present will receive a _____ **2**

This will be forwarded by _____ **3**

The two topics for discussion today are the

_____ **4** and how to study for the course.

How many TMAs are there? _____ **5**

TMAs must not be _____ **6**

You can treat specified word length as

_____ **7**

If possible, TMAs should be _____ **8**

Tutors will make comments on the TMA and in a

_____ **9**

At the end of the TMA students should include

_____ **10**

Tip Strip

Remember:

• check whether you must answer with a letter, a number, a word or a short phrase.

• notice that the rubric specifies the length of the answers.

Question 11: Think in advance of the kind of accidents that could happen and then listen for the right one.

Question 12: Although you hear this only once, the information may be repeated in a slightly different way. Listen for this.

Question 13: How many types of train are there? (Not very many)

Question 14: Think of how a railway is described. Probably with the names of the cities it goes to and from.

You will hear a radio announcement about travel problems on the railway. For questions **11–20**, complete the notes according to the information you hear, using one or two words or a time.

Listen very carefully as you will hear the recording ONCE only.

Travel News

Kind of accident: | 11

Time of accident: | 12

Type of train involved: | 13

Name of the blocked line: | 14

People injured: | 15

Cause of accident: | 16

Trains subject to delay:

Travellers from South Wales will arrive

| 17

For travellers from Gloucester to Swindon, everything is

| 18

Travellers from Bath to Paddington will arrive

| 19

Travellers to Wales will find the journey takes

| 20

You will hear a radio interview with a researcher, Shirley Grainger, who has been investigating the working situation of actresses. For questions **21–30**, complete the statements.

You will hear the recording twice.

Actresses at Work

Compared to men, the roles actresses play represent people who are

	21

The survey was commissioned by

	22

It covered three places of work:

	23
	24
	25

As well as gender, age and type of role, researchers investigated

	26

The survey found that male actors are busiest when they are

	27

In order to be well-paid for radio jobs, it is essential to have

	28

With regard to lack of parts for women, producers blame

	29

In the afternoon, most of the people listening to drama are

	30

Tip Strip

Remember:
• although it is best to do Task One on the first listening and Task Two on the second listening, you should read Task Two before you listen the first time.
• for Task Two listen for the attitude of the speaker.

Task One
B: What words do you associate with the job of secretary, etc.? Do you hear any of them in the first extract?

Task Two
B: What words do you expect to hear in connection with financial changes?

You will hear **five** short extracts in which different people talk about losing jobs.

Losing Your Job

TASK ONE

For questions **31–35**, match the extracts as you hear them with the professions, listed **A–H**.

A   TV star

B   secretary

C   bank clerk

D   therapist

E   drama producer

F   employer

G   advertising executive

H   council employee

	31
	32
	33
	34
	35

TASK TWO

For questions **36–40**, match the extracts as you hear them with the statements about the speakers, listed **A–H**.

A   appreciates a positive approach

B   has made financial changes

C   advocates adopting a routine

D   was disappointed about monetary arrangements

E   expects to get a job soon

F   has come to terms with the situation

G   was given some warning of what was to happen

H   admits to benefiting from the experience

	36
	37
	38
	39
	40

Remember that you must complete both tasks as you listen. You will hear the recording twice.

Guide to PAPER 5 Speaking

PAPER 5 consists of four parts. There are two students and two examiners. One examiner communicates with the students and the other concentrates on assessment. During the test students talk with the examiner, with each other and individually. Pictures and other visual prompts are used to stimulate discussion.

This paper tests your ability to describe and comment on visuals, to negotiate and collaborate with your partner, and to summarise and develop conclusions.

Part 1: Social Interaction (page 33)

The examiners will introduce themselves then ask whether you and your partner know each other. They will invite you to ask each other general questions on topics such as your interests, current studies or job, or future plans.

In this part you should:
- ask and answer general information questions.
- talk about your current job, studies, interests, living conditions or plans for the future.
- express opinions about any of these topics.

Part 2: Individual Long Turn (page 33)

You talk for one minute without interruption, in response to photographs, diagrams or cartoons. You then make a brief (20 second) comment on the other candidate's photographs after he / she has spoken for one minute.

In this part you should:
- compare and contrast what you can see in the pictures, and the ideas suggested by them.
- give reasons for, and explanations of, the situations shown in the photos and related situations and topics.
- talk about possibilities, what might have happened and what could happen in the future.
- comment briefly on the pictures that the other candidate speaks about for one minute.
- not interrupt the other candidate.

Part 3: Collaborative Task (page 33)

You and your partner discuss a decision-making / problem-solving task, illustrated by visual material, without interruption by the examiner. The task may involve speculating or prioritising.

In this part you should:
- give your own opinions and listen to those of the other candidate.
- explain and justify your opinions.
- make suggestions and discuss possibilities.

- agree or disagree, giving reasons.
- reach an agreed decision or agree to disagree.

Part 4: Discussion (page 33)

Part 4 is an extension of Part 3. The same task is discussed but now the examiner joins in the discussion.

In this part you should do everything you did in Part 3, and also:
- summarise your discussion.
- develop points further in response to the examiner's comments.

Exam tips

- Listen carefully to questions asked by the examiners and your partner.
- Show interest in what your partner is saying.
- Do not say that you 'don't know' about a particular topic. Try to find something relevant to say.
- Do not try to rehearse what you will say because this will be obvious to the examiners. They may interrupt you with questions that require unrehearsed answers.
- Do not worry if you think your partner is much better or worse than you. The examiners are not comparing you with your partner. They are giving you each a separate mark according to the assessment criteria.
- If you do not understand something, ask for clarification. Carrying out the task depends on your understanding what the examiner has asked you to do.

How is the Speaking Paper marked?

You are given marks for:

Grammar and Vocabulary: This refers to the accurate and appropriate use of grammar and vocabulary. The range of vocabulary used is also assessed.

Discourse Management: This includes student's ability to express ideas and opinions in coherent, connected speech. Students are expected to express or justify opinions using a range of linguistic structures.

Pronunciation: This refers to student's ability to produce comprehensible English, as well as the natural linking of words, and the use of stress and intonation to convey meaning.

Interactive Communication: This applies to Parts 1 and 3 and focuses on student's ability to take turns and participate actively in discussions.

PAPER 5   Speaking (15 minutes)

Tip Strip

- Don't panic if you are given a picture and you do not know the words to describe what is in it. Use paraphrase and expressions such as 'the thing in the corner', 'the stuff he's carrying' and 'the thing used for … +ing'.

Part 3

- Co-operate with your partner. Take turns and provide opportunities for your partner to continue speaking on the same topic. Ask questions or make statements that invite a response.

PART 1   (3 minutes)

The examiner gets both candidates to talk briefly about themselves by asking questions such as:

How do you travel to work / college?
Are you satisfied with the public transport system in this town?
What is your favourite form of transport and why?

PART 2   (3 or 4 minutes)

You each talk for one minute without interruption in response to a visual prompt. You are encouraged to make a brief comment after your partner has spoken.

The World of Work (Describe and comment)

Turn to pictures 1–3 on page 129 which show people working very hard.

Candidate A, describe what they are doing and why you think they are working in this way. You have a minute to do this.

Candidate B, in which photograph do you think people are working hardest?

Living Dangerously (Describe and comment)

Turn to pictures 1–2 on page 130 which show people in dangerous situations.

Candidate B, compare and contrast these situations, saying how you think they happened. You have a minute to do this.

Candidate A, which situation do you think is the most dangerous?

PART 3   (3 or 4 minutes)

You both discuss a decision-making / problem-solving task, illustrated by visual material, without interruption by the examiner.

Freetime Activities (Prioritise and discuss)

Turn to pictures 1–5 on page 131 taken from a leaflet about a one-month summer course to study English in England. It shows some of the things that students could do when classes have finished. If only three of these activities can be provided, which do you think students would prefer?

PART 4   (3 or 4 minutes)

The examiner encourages you to develop the discussion in Part 3 by asking questions such as:

Did you reach agreement?
How do your opinions differ?
Do you think the age of students makes any difference?
Are there any other activities you would recommend for such a course?

TEST 2

PAPER 1

Reading (1 hour 15 minutes)

PART 1

Answer questions **1–16** by referring to the newspaper article about sportsmen on page **35**.

Indicate your answers **on the separate answer sheet**.

Tip Strip

Remember:
- highlight key words and phrases in the questions, such as 'dangerous incident' or 'another career'. You will find these words, or words expressing the same idea, in the text.
- highlight the names in the questions and in the text. This will help you find the information quickly.

Question 6: What kind of things can 'domestic difficulties' refer to?
Question 9: What experiences might make a sportsman feel like an outsider?
Question 11: What events could end a sports career suddenly?

For questions **1–16**, answer by choosing from the list (**A–F**) on the right below.

Some of the choices may be required more than once.

Which person

describes a very dangerous incident?	**1** ....
helps other sportsmen adjust to the ending of their careers?	**2** ....
seems to have experienced the least difficulty?	**3** ....
said something that left an interviewer speechless?	**4** ....
appeared to be someone who would cope well with the end of his sports career?	**5** ....
experienced domestic difficulties?	**6** ....
returned to his sport after trying other things?	**7** ....
felt angry at no longer being a star?	**8** ....
felt a sense of being an outsider?	**9** ....
says that ex-sportsmen may have to start new jobs at the lowest level?	**10** ....
experienced a sudden and unexpected end to his career?	**11** ....
received accurate advice from his coach?	**12** ....
compares leaving his sport to the death of a relative?	**13** ....
returned to his sport and then found another career?	**14** ....
was replaced in his team by someone else?	**15** ....
mentions a possible loss of income?	**16** ....

A Stan Bowles

B Rodney Marsh

C Bob Latchford

D Frank Bruno

E Brendan Batson

F John Watson

THEY THINK IT'S ALL OVER

N sport, the fall from stardom can be hard and sudden. Some come to a tragic end, others drift happily into mundane jobs.

Retirement was never a problem for Stan Bowles. When he chatted to Cliff Morgan about his life and career, Morgan asked him how much he missed the adulation, the glory, the limelight of professional sport. Had he felt lonely? "Well," said Bowles. "I know it does take a lot of players like that. But you have to remember I had my betting to fall back on." Morgan was silent.

One of Bowles's team-mates in 1970s football, Rodney Marsh, was outwardly prepared for the transition – more successful, an intelligent man with a chance to do a host of things outside or inside the game – but he wasn't as happy-go-lucky as Bowles. He tells of driving his car down the Cromwell Road after he had packed in the game. He got to a red light. "I just thought 'Why not?' and put my foot down. I was hoping something was coming the other way and would crash into me. I just had no idea what I was going to do."

The problems sportsmen face once they have to get to grips with real life after a career as part of a team are very real. Some even go as far as killing themselves. The anger in Frank Bruno's eyes as he increasingly lost his temper at home and which forced his wife to seek a court order against him is, say some sports psychologists, part of the same problem – the frustration of not being important, of not being the focus, of having to get to grips with the mundane reality of normal life. "When I came out of boxing, it was like a bereavement," says Bruno. "Every morning, I had got out of bed at 6am to train, even on Christmas Day, and now I was getting up with nothing to do. My trainer once warned me that the toughest fight I would ever have would be out of the ring adjusting to life, and he was right. I had so many confused thoughts, I didn't know which way to turn. I went into self-destruct."

The problem for many sports people is that they never quite get around to planning for the day when the floodlights go out. But in sport, the fall can be hard and sudden. John Watson was one of Britain's leading Formula One drivers until 1983 when he was suddenly dropped by McLaren in favour of Alain Prost. "You try to put it off, you try not to think about it, though you know it can happen," says Watson. "And it hurts when suddenly you are not part of it all any more. When I went back to a Grand Prix in Belgium in 1984, I walked into the paddock and felt like a stranger, like I just didn't belong here any more even after ten years in the game. I came away in a not very good emotional state." Watson was lucky, he drove for Jaguar in sportscar racing and is now a successful broadcaster.

The problem is worse, though, for those whose life has been played out in a team from 16 to 35. "The trouble is that you never imagine yourself not as a player," says Bob Latchford, Everton and England football centre-forward of the 1970s. "You may never see the possibility that one day you won't be part of it. Even if you've thought about it, being dropped into the real world still comes as a shock. Mentally, it's very hard to cope with the fact that you've got to do something else for the next 30-odd years." Latchford struggled for a while. He ran a childrenswear business. Then he worked for a company that runs betting shops and then got back into the game as a youth coach at Birmingham City Football Club.

For the modern footballer, though, things are much better. Since 1984, the Professional Footballers Association has run an education scheme to prepare players for the outside world. "For sportsmen, the problem is that they are finishing a career at 35," says Brendan Batson of the PFA, "they are often having to start at the bottom rung of other professional ladders where their contemporaries are often 15 years ahead of them. Often they have to take a pay cut, too, for which they aren't prepared." Batson's own career was ended at 31 by injury. "That is hard," he says, "because you don't have time to adjust." ■

For questions **17–22**, you must choose which of paragraphs **A–G** on page **37** fit into the numbered gaps in the following newspaper article. There is one extra paragraph which does not fit in any of the gaps.

Indicate your answers **on the separate answer sheet**.

A TOWN LIKE DAVIS

DAVIS, near Sacramento, in California, has a population of forty thousand. It also has forty thousand bicycles and just nine thousand cars. Cyclists have right of way everywhere in the town, seventy kilometres of bike lanes all to themselves, and their own unit of specially trained cycle police. The American obsession with the motor car would seem to have been tamed, at least in this one small corner of the USA.

17

As a university town, Davis has always had more than its fair share of bicycles – and of ecological awareness too. It is home to the University of California's Faculty of Agriculture, and back in the early seventies, a group of students and local people got together to draw up a comprehensive environmental and social plan of action to steer Davis away from the terminal urban sprawl that afflicts so many other American cities.

18

Energy saving is at the top of this local agenda, and by the year 2000, the people of Davis expect the Californian sun to be providing half of all their energy needs. In pursuit of this objective, the town council has introduced many regulations which are designed to keep energy use to the absolute minimum.

19

This is a very quaint custom by American standards! The majority of people have taken to sorting out their household waste into different piles, separating paper, metal and plastic, for example, so that specially designed dust carts can take it away for recycling.

20

The size of building plots has been drastically reduced, so housing densities are high and there is enough room left over to make cheap allotments available to all flat owners without a garden.

21

There are popular street markets twice a week where locally grown produce is bought and sold, giving everyone a chance to enjoy fresh food and to plough profits straight back into neighbouring farms.

Two long-term residents of the town, Jan and Jim Hogan, told an interesting story of how, when their daughter was in her teens, she could hardly wait to head out of Davis and make a life for herself in the big city. But now she is back in the town where she grew up, with her husband and small son in tow, because she could not think of a better place to raise her own family.

22

Given such a track record, it should not come as a surprise that the vast majority of people in Davis support the changes that have been made.

A Planning by-laws in Davis are based on the premise that a 'green city' is not a contradiction in terms. Houses are restricted to two storeys and business premises to four.

B This kind of personal story is not surprising: Davis has no slums, no ghettos, very little unemployment and the lowest crime rate in the United States. People leave their doors unlocked. It actually works!

C It is we 'townies' who are the ones with the most to gain by putting the notion of 'the environment' firmly at the centre of our lives – in terms of the air we breathe, the water we drink, the quality of our food and the conviviality of our communities.

D The fact that one hundred and fifty bicycles take up the same space as twenty cars means that they have been busily turning car-parks into green oases rather than the other way around.

E At forty square metres, one of these allotments can provide seventy per cent of all fruit and veg for a two-person household if properly managed. Organically managed, that is – for Davis is pretty much a pesticide-free town.

F Three of the students got themselves elected to the city council and initiated a flow of legislation that has affected every aspect of local life since then. One of those students, Bill Carter, is the current mayor of the town.

G Strict building standards are enforced and thousands of trees have been planted to discourage people from installing air-conditioning. The trees provide shade exactly where it is most needed. People in Davis even hang out their washing to dry instead of throwing it in the tumble dryer.

Tip Strip

Remember to:
- highlight words that refer to people, places and events.
- look for clues before and after the gaps.

Question 17: The key words are 'cars' and 'bicycles'. Which paragraph makes this link?

Question 21: Which paragraph makes a link between gardens and growing food?

Question 22: Which paragraph refers to the story of the Hogan family?

Read the following article from a journal and then answer questions **23–29** on page **39**. On your answer sheet, indicate the letter **A**, **B**, **C** or **D** against the number of each question, **23–29**. Give only one answer to each question.

Indicate your answers **on the separate answer sheet**.

Whales

'The whale has no voice', wrote Melville in Moby Dick 'but then again what has the whale to say? Seldom have I known any profound being that had anything to say to this world, unless to stammer out something by way of getting a living.' Not so. Whales may not sing for their suppers, but some of them certainly do sing. Melville failed to hear them because they sing underwater. Others have heard them without realising it. If whales sing near a wooden-bottomed boat, sailors in their bunks or hammocks may hear an eerie melodious wail from they know not where. Hence, perhaps, the many sea-tales of lullabies sung by drowned colleagues.

Why do they sing? First, spot the singers. There are two sorts of whales: the toothed whales – such as sperm, killer and pilot whales – who are close relatives of the porpoise and the dolphin; and the toothless 'baleen' whales – such as the humpback, right and minke. The toothed whales usually live in stable and organised groups: a gang of killer whales may stay together for years on end. Such creatures make sounds, but have not been known to sing. Many dolphins produce 'signature' whistles – each one has a different call-sign from his neighbours. These seem to function as names: a dolphin will often produce his neighbour's whistle when nearby. Similarly, each sperm whale produces a distinctive series of clicks – known as his coda – and will sometimes mimic a nearby whale's coda. Killer whales have identifiable dialects that are specific to each family. It is the baleen whales, especially the humpbacks, who break into song. At any one time, all the singing whales in a population sing the same song. It gradually changes over time and each whale learns and copies the new variations. This is a formidable feat because the songs, which can last up to thirty minutes, are highly complex. It is only the males who sing, and they do so chiefly during the breeding season. The songs seem – like many bird songs – to be a sort of display that males use in competing with each other for females.

Singing humpbacks have a wide vocal range: the notes can swoop down from a high-pitched factory whistle to a reverberating fog-horn. Play back a recorded humpback song at fourteen times the correct speed and it sounds like a nightingale. But birdsong is shorter – and more significantly – not so structured as whale song. Whale song can be broken down into regularly repeating phrases, which in turn are organised into themes that always occur in the same sequence. Unlike birds, whales appear to have studied some of the rules of classical composition.

By analysing these themes and phrases, two scientists have reached conclusions about whale culture that would have struck Melville dumb. Whales seem to use a structure like rhyme in poetry. And, like people, they may put in the rhymes to help them remember their songs. The two scientists, Miss Linda Guinee of the Long Term Research Institute in Lincoln, Massachusetts, and Mrs Katharine Payne of Cornell University in Ithaca, New York, analysed 460 whale songs from the North Pacific and 88 from the North Atlantic. From their recordings they produced audio spectograms, converting sounds into strings of squiggles which can be classified by shape. Having a catalogue of whale songs helps marine biologists to track whale populations on their odysseys by showing where each singer comes from. It also lets them study the songs as they evolve. Since whales learn their songs, such songs are an example of culture; and the way they change is an example of cultural evolution.

It turns out that whales make much use of phrases with the same endings – i.e. rhymes. Miss Guinee and Mrs Payne found that songs with many differing themes were much more likely to contain plenty of rhymes. They found that rhymes were correlated not with the length of a song but with the amount of different material to be remembered. Simple songs did not contain any rhyming passages. The rhyming pattern then, could be a way to help the whale remember what comes next in a complicated song. A rhyming pattern helps people to learn and remember poetry by limiting the number of possible words in a given position. If you know that every third and fourth line of a stanza in a given poem rhyme, and that the third line of a stanza ends with 'love', you know that the next line might end with 'dove' but cannot end with 'sparrow'. Advertising jingles often use rhyme in the justified hope that people will remember the names of products. You do not have to know the meaning of a word or sign in order for rhyme to help you recall it (think of children's nonsense rhymes). Poets use rhyme for all sorts of reasons: because they are attractive, musical, create a pleasing rhythm, or are merely ingenious or funny.

Miss Guinee and Mrs Payne realise that their evidence is inconclusive, because they cannot ask the whales what they are up to. Some will doubt their conclusion because it makes whales seem implausibly human. Maybe they have not made whales 'human' enough. Perhaps the rhyming sirens of the deep are simply trying to please themselves and their audience.

23 What did Melville believe about whales?

    A They didn't produce vocal sounds.
    B They had nothing to say.
    C They couldn't imitate the human voice.
    D They couldn't sing.

24 Which of the following seem to use personal identification signals?

    A killer whales
    B porpoises
    C sperm whales
    D baleen whales

25 What is known about the song of a humpback whale?

    A It is identical to that of a nightingale.
    B It could be taken for birdsong if it was slower.
    C It mimics sounds produced by musical instruments.
    D It is rather more complex than that of birds.

26 Why does the writer say 'Whales appear to have studied some of the rules of classical composition'?

    A He believes whales are more intelligent than most people think.
    B He doesn't take the research seriously.
    C He thinks there is evidence that whales have learnt through contact with humans.
    D He is trying to amuse his readers.

27 What did the two scientists discover?

    A There were four hundred and sixty types of whale song.
    B Whale song varied according to how fast the whales were travelling.
    C Whales responded when music was played to them.
    D The songs demonstrated where the whales originated from.

28 Where are rhymes most likely to occur?

    A in songs which are being learnt
    B in complicated songs
    C in songs which have changed
    D in long songs

29 What is the conclusion of the writer of the article?

    A That the scientists want to make whales appear too much like humans.
    B That the scientific work on whales is too inconclusive to be taken seriously.
    C That scientists may be missing a simple and obvious explanation for whale song.
    D That scientists may have found a way of communicating with whales.

Tip Strip

Remember:
- skim read the text for general understanding.
- underline key words in the questions and options.

Question 23: Sometimes the text and the question use different words for the same idea. Which words in the text mean 'didn't produce vocal sounds'?

Question 24: If you have highlighted these different types of whales in the text, it will help you to find the information you need.

Tip Strip

Remember:

• go through each section of the text in turn (e.g. A – Rose Tremain), matching questions which refer to it. By the time you get to the sixth section, you will have nearly all the answers.

• Make links between different pieces of information in the text. In the section on Fitzroy Maclean, for example, what is the link between '1946' and 'typewriter' and 'Never again'?

Answer questions **30–49** by referring to the information writers give about themselves on pages **41–42**.

Indicate your answers **on the separate answer sheet**.

For questions **30–49** choose your answers from the list of writers (**A–F**) on the right below.

Some choices may be required more than once.

Note: When more than one answer is required, these may be given **in any order**.

Which writer(s)

admits to being able to work anywhere?	**30**		
refer to someone who helps with the typing?	**31**	**32**	
has used a word processor?	**33**		
can only work when the room is a particular temperature?	**34**		**A** Rose Tremain
uses a typewriter?	**35**		**B** Patrick Gale
used a typewriter in the past?	**36**	**37**	**C** Jilly Cooper
undertakes domestic duties before settling down to write?	**38**		**D** Julian Barnes
experiences initial resistance to starting work?	**39**		**E** Susan Hill
enjoy frequent coffee breaks?	**40**	**41**	**F** Sir Fitzroy Maclean
mentions the need for peace and quiet?	**42**		
refers to a previous working routine?	**43**		
have more than one workplace?	**44**	**45**	
doesn't stop for lunch?	**46**		
exercises indoors?	**47**		
watch TV to relax?	**48**	**49**	

Writers Do It Lying Down!

How and where do writers write? With coffee and cacophony or in austere silence? In warm kitchens or in lonely attics? Joanna Trollop follows the muse of successful novelists.

Rose Tremain

I've got the study I've always longed for. It looks out onto a big sloping lawn, and as soon as I go into it in the morning, it just takes me in. I like to start the day slowly, giving external attention to breakfast but some internal attention to the writing day ahead. I'm at my desk by ten. I like to be alone then and I like silence. I hate winter. My study has to be at least 70 degrees or I can't concentrate. I write in longhand with Berol Mirado pencils on recycled paper. I'm aware of the need to be fit and well so I eat conscientiously at lunchtime. I stop at 5.30, do exactly 35 minutes of yoga, put on some Mozart or Haydn, and play around with food, which is a wonderful way of engaging other senses than the ones I use all day.

Patrick Gale

One of the joys of being a writer is that you don't have to have a routine, but when I've got a book on the boil I really don't do anything else. My brain only works until lunchtime and food is vital to keep me going: digestive biscuits are a must and I do confess to the odd chocolate crisis. I work until I'm really hungry, and then I take the dog out to thrash out any problems. After lunch, I'll read — mostly novels by dead authors so as not to get too demoralised. If it's warm, I work in a summerhouse I built, which has a view of the garden. If it's very cold, I shut myself into the loft. I have to confess I work better there. It's where the word processor lives, although I like to work with pencil and exercise book first, to tease ideas out. The evenings are for the box. I love it. I video old films. That's my treat.

Jilly Cooper

When I'm on a book, I'll work all day, every day. I start about ten, and I'll go on and on, until eight or nine. There's nothing in the middle except a dog walk and a chat to the horses. There's not even any food really, because I'm always trying to lose weight. The room where I work is serious chaos. The room faces south, so my typist Monica and I trek about to whichever surface has no sun and the least mess. I keep longhand notebooks of all the events and characters in the current book and a file for each chapter. If Leo's here, it's great, because he'll usually cook supper. By then I'm only fit to slump in front of the telly.

Julian Barnes

When I get to my desk at about ten, I find I don't very much want to be there. Luckily, this feeling passes. My desk is in a light, upstairs room painted Chinese yellow. There are two prunus trees outside, which bullfinches seem to like, and once I saw a jay. I'm fairly easily distracted, and will roam off to get mugs of coffee, biscuits and raisins, and wait hopefully by the letter box for the postman. The best creative time is from ten to one. I work on a big black electric typewriter. I don't want a word processor. When I'm working on a novel, I'll put in a seven-day week. Cooking's helpful if I'm stuck. I don't really reward myself at the end of a good day. I'm just relieved to feel less guilty.

Susan Hill

When I was single, I had a lovely long morning that began at about eight, with nobody to think about but me. There's no doubt it's harder now, having got up at 6.30 and done the school run, and having one's head seething with domestic things. You have to guard against that dangerous, restless time when you return home and can get waylaid so easily. I'm working in a Portakabin in the garden while we convert a barn into my study. I take coffee in there and sit quietly, thinking myself down into the book again. I have little breaks for more coffee, but this doesn't interfere with concentration at all, nor does my stunning view. I stop at lunchtime and that's it really. I use jumbo economy pads and write in longhand. I prefer pencil. I used to type the manuscript myself but then I found a wonderful lady who can read my writing. I'm useless with machines and their noise would drown the words in my head.

Sir Fitzroy Maclean

I wrote Eastern Approaches 45 years ago, and I've had a book on the go ever since. I travel all the time and I get on with writing wherever I am, buses, helicopters, airports, anywhere. In 1946, in America, I bought a portable typewriter but when I'd typed 150,000 words on it, I thought, 'Never again.' I like yellow spiral-backed pads and those floating ball pens. My ideal is to write in the library, or in my specially insulated room at home in Scotland, or at the kitchen table in London, sustaining myself with a huge pot of China tea. If I'm travelling, I take a flask for tea – it's vital. I like regular meals and I'm inclined to sleep after lunch. My book is my first thought every day, and it's my escape from real life. I don't need a reward at the end of a day. The writing is a prize in itself.

PART 1

1   You are studying in Oxford and recently went to your friend Fiona's birthday party in Scotland. You have known her for a long time and helped to organise the party. The other day you received a letter from her. Read the letter below and the newspaper advertisement you saw in the Oxford Mail. Then, **using the information carefully**, write **a letter** to your friend Fiona, giving whatever advice you think best.

Write approximately 250 words. You should use your own words as far as possible. It is not necessary to include addresses.

Oxford Mail
Tuesday 5 March

CLASSIFIED ADVERTISEMENTS

FOR SALE
GEORGE III SILVER TEAPOT

Perfect condition
Must sell immediately
£1500 for quick sale –
a bargain at this price
Cash only

Phone Oxford 623980 and
ask for Mick

Dear _____

It was great to see you the other weekend and I really appreciated you coming all the way to Inverness to help me organise my birthday party. There were more people there than I expected so I really needed an extra pair of hands. Everyone had a wonderful time, I'm sure you'll agree, but unfortunately something has happened which is causing me a lot of worry.

As you know, because you must have heard me mention it, my father is a keen collector of antique silver – in fact, he's quite an expert on it. Well, when Mum and Dad got back from their weekend away they were very pleased that the house was clean and tidy and back to normal but then, to his horror, my father discovered that the cabinet in which he keeps his silver had been forced open and a valuable George III silver teapot was missing – it's worth about £2,000 apparently. There were no signs of a break-in, so it very much looks as if one of the party guests stole it. Of course, most of them were my friends who, I'm sure wouldn't do anything like that, but some were friends of friends and people I didn't really know very well. I'm wondering if you heard or saw anything suspicious at the party, anything at all that might help to give us a clue. I do hope you can help.

Actually, I tried to phone you last night but you must have been out. I did get through to Michael (his number is 623980 if you want to get in touch) who, like you, is already back in Oxford, but he hadn't seen anything suspicious. By the way, Michael and I are engaged to be married. We were going to announce it at my party, but Michael said he couldn't afford to buy me an engagement ring yet so we should delay the announcement until he could.

Let me know if you have anything to tell me. I'm so depressed about this teapot business. I'll be in Oxford in about two weeks.

Love
Fiona

Tip Strip

Question 1: This is a letter to a friend so start 'Dear Fiona' and end (for example) 'Best wishes' and then sign with your first name only.
You have to advise Fiona, but it is entirely up to you to decide what advice to give. Make some notes on your ideas before you start writing. You need to refer to what you saw at the party, to the information in Fiona's letter and to the advertisement that you have seen. Then you have to draw your own conclusions.

Choose one of the following writing tasks. Your answer should follow exactly the instructions given. Write approximately 250 words.

Tip Strip

Question 2: This is a letter to a company, so start 'Dear Sir or Madam' and end 'Yours faithfully'. Alternatively, invent a name for the manager of the company and start 'Dear Mr Brown' and end 'Yours sincerely.'
Your opening sentence must make it clear why you are writing – to make suggestions about the leisure centre. Give reasons for each suggestion you make.

Question 3: Make sure you deal with both topics – theft and vandalism. Suggest improvement measures that relate directly to these problems such as employing security guards, installing security cameras, checking student's identity cards, etc.

Question 4: A review normally has the name of the book and the author at the top. In this case, you could write the original title and an English translation. Briefly summarise the content of the book, then outline the reasons you are recommending it.

2 In the town in Britain where you are studying at a language school, there is a proposal to build a Sports and Leisure Centre providing a range of sports and leisure facilities. The company which is going to build the centre wishes to know what facilities (e.g. swimming, weight-training, tennis, martial arts, etc.) will be most popular. You have carried out a survey among the students at your school and have studied their opinions and suggestions concerning sports facilities, prices and opening hours. Write to the company summarising the suggestions that have been made.

Write your **letter**.

3 In the college where you are studying, there have been several cases of theft in recent weeks. Students have lost personal belongings, and items of equipment such as computers and cassette-players have been stolen. There have also been acts of vandalism. Students have held a meeting to discuss ways of improving security in the college. Send a report to the principal of the college with your recommendations.

Write your **report**.

4 The editor of a student magazine in Britain has asked you to write a review (in English) of a book (in your own language). The book should be suitable for students who are learning your language and have reached a high standard, but are not totally fluent. Choose an appropriate book and say why you recommend it. The book may be a novel, a biography, a true-life adventure, etc. Do not choose a book specially written for foreign students.

Write your **review**.

5 In the building where you work you have special responsibility for health and safety. You have identified two potential safety problems. Write a report to the manager, explaining which aspects of the building and / or working practices may be unsafe and suggesting what should be done to improve things.

Write your **report**.

Question 5: This is a report, so choose the correct layout. Remember you have to write about two things only, e.g. overcrowded eating and drinking areas, poor access to emergency exits, etc. For each one, you must describe the problem and suggest a solution. You can use sub-headings in your report.

PART 1

For questions **1–15**, read the text below and then decide which word best fits each space. Put the letter you choose for each question in the correct box on your answer sheet. The exercise begins with an example (**0**).

Example: 0   D   0

That Sweet Smell of Success is ...

There is a revolution in the retail world that cannot (**0**) .... to attract shoppers' noses. In the latest marketing ploy, smells are created in laboratories to be wafted around stores in order to (**1**) .... the unsuspecting into spending more money. Secret (**2**) .... of the 'designer' smells are going on in more than a hundred stores across Britain, including bookshops, petrol stations and a (**3**) .... of clothes shops. The tailor-made aromas (**4**) .... coconut oil in travel agents (to (**5**) .... exotic holidays), and leather in car showrooms (to suggest (**6**) .... quality). Marketing Aromatics, a company specialising in this area, believes that odours are under-used as a marketing (**7**) .... . Until now the most frequent (**8**) .... has been in supermarkets where the smell from in-store bakeries has been blown among the (**9**) .... to boost sales of fresh food. 'We are taking things one stage further,' said David Fellowes, the company's commercial director. 'We can build on customer loyalty by making customers (**10**) .... a particular smell with a particular store. It is not intrusive. If it were it would defeat the (**11**) .... .'

The smells are designed to work on three levels: to relax shoppers by using natural smells such as peppermint; to bring back memories using odours such as a whiff of sea breeze; and to encourage customer loyalty by using a corporate perfume 'logo' to (**12**) .... a company's image. Dr George Dodd, scientific adviser to Marketing Aromatics, believes smells can affect people's moods. 'It is a very exciting time. Smells have enormous (**13**) .... to influence behaviour,' he said. Critics say retailers are (**14**) .... to subliminal advertising. 'Not telling consumers that this is happening is an (**15**) .... invasion of their privacy. People have the right to know,' said Conor Foley of Liberty, the civil liberties association.

0	**A** manage	**B** stop	**C** work	**D** fail
1	**A** entice	**B** trap	**C** force	**D** deceive
2	**A** investigations	**B** analyses	**C** operations	**D** trials
3	**A** society	**B** chain	**C** company	**D** network
4	**A** include	**B** cover	**C** spread	**D** spray
5	**A** remember	**B** arouse	**C** evoke	**D** desire
6	**A** complete	**B** expensive	**C** lasting	**D** permanent
7	**A** advertisement	**B** tool	**C** gadget	**D** gimmick
8	**A** effect	**B** concept	**C** type	**D** application
9	**A** aisles	**B** gangways	**C** corridors	**D** walkways
10	**A** join	**B** associate	**C** bond	**D** merge
11	**A** target	**B** method	**C** object	**D** thing
12	**A** make	**B** fix	**C** show	**D** express
13	**A** concentration	**B** strength	**C** potential	**D** ability
14	**A** resorting	**B** taking	**C** moving	**D** reacting
15	**A** undeserving	**B** unjustified	**C** unofficial	**D** unlicensed

Tip Strip

Question 16: This is clearly a question, so which auxiliary verb is missing?

Question 19: This is not a new sentence, so the answer is not 'it'. Which word can be a substitute for 'it'?

Question 25: The second part of the sentence explains how something happens. Which preposition does this?

For questions **16–30** complete the following article by writing each missing word in the correct box on your answer sheet. **Use only one word for each space.** The exercise begins with an example (**0**).

Example:

0	*or*		0
			☐ ▬

Volcanoes: Dangers and Benefits

There are fifteen capital cities in the world in a position to be wiped out (**0**) .... seriously damaged by volcanic eruptions. So why then (**16**) .... people continue to live in (**17**) .... dangerous areas? Many of these people are poor and have (**18**) .... choice, while others disregard the risk, (**19**) .... is, after all, rather (**20**) .... than the risks involved in smoking or driving a car. What attracts people to volcanic areas (**21**) .... fertile land. The soils from volcanic ashes are light, easily worked, drain well and are full (**22**) .... plant nutrients. A light fall of ash, (**23**) .... it may destroy one year's crop, often pays the farmer (**24**) .... in future years (**25**) .... the fertility it adds to the soil. Coffee in Colombia, vines in Italy and rice in Japan are (**26**) .... a few of the crops that flourish on volcanic soils.

In Italy, Japan, New Zealand, the United States and Iceland the subterranean heat from volcanoes (**27**) .... used in geothermal power stations to generate electricity. In many places, the way in which the flows of lava concentrate minerals (**28**) .... them attractive to mining companies. There is growing evidence that gold is (**29**) .... the minerals collected by volcanic flows, and the diamond-mining industry in South Africa takes advantage of the huge pressures within past volcanoes (**30**) .... have produced diamonds.

PART 3

Tip Strip

- If a comma, full stop or bracket is missing, write it with the two words on either side. If these punctuation marks are unnecessary, write the two words on either side but not the mark itself.
- If the mistake is to do with spelling, capital or small letters, an apostrophe or hyphen, write that one word correctly.

Line 31: Is the comma correct?

Line 32: What part of the verb is 'chose'? What parts are 'choose' and 'chosen'?

Line 33: What is the rule for 'ie' and 'ei' spellings?

Line 35: Sometimes words with silent letters can be misspelt.

Line 37: What is the difference between 'advice' and 'advise'? Which one is a verb and which a noun? Which one can go with 'some'?

Line 41: Brackets always come in pairs. Check that both are present.

Line 42: Check where sentences begin and end. Are there capital letters and full stops?

In **most** lines of the following text, there is either a spelling or a punctuation error. For each numbered line **31–46**, write the correctly spelled word(s) or show the correct punctuation in the box on your answer sheet. Some lines are correct. Indicate these lines with a tick (✓) in the box. The exercise begins with three examples (**0**).

Examples:

0	✓	0
00	*didn't*	0
000	*lose*	0

Going it Alone

0	....	When he was made redundant four years ago, John Spencer set up his own
00	....	business dealing in rare and second-hand books. "I didnt expect to
000	....	loose my job," he said. "It happened very suddenly and I knew it would
31	....	be difficult to find another one, I'd always been interested in books,
32	....	so that seemed a good business to chose. I run the business from home
33	....	and send and recieve books by post so I don't need my own premises.
34	....	Sometimes I travell to book fairs and sometimes I have a stall in the
35	....	market. It was a bit frigtening at first, being self-employed, but I've
36	....	got used to it now and I really appreciate the feeling of independence I
37	....	get from being my own boss." John got some advise from his bank
38	....	manager about the financial aspects of his business and also took out a
39	....	small lone to buy stock. After only two years the business was making a
40	....	profit. The secret of sucess, according to John, is to specialise in
41	....	certain areas (detective fiction and cookery in his case so that you
42	....	always have the book the serious collector is looking for John posts
43	....	books to his customers and then waits for them to send payment. At
44	....	first he wasn't sure wether people would pay up promptly. "In fact,
45	....	this hasnt been the problem I thought it might be. Most customers are
46	....	very honest and its only the occasional one that causes problems."

Tip Strip

- Identify the part of speech given and think of the other forms of that word.

Question 47: What is the noun?

Question 52: What kind of prefix do you need? How many changes do you need to make?

Question 53: Is this singular or plural?

Question 54: What spelling change do you need to make?

Question 59: What is the prefix?

Question 60: Do you need a double letter?

For questions **47–61** read the two texts below. Use the words in the boxes to the right of the texts to form **one** word that fits in the same numbered space in the text. The exercise begins with an example (**0**).

Example:

0	*responsibility*	0

NOTICE

IN CASE OF FIRE

General Instructions

In an emergency, the first (**0**) .... of all members of staff is to prevent injury or (**47**) .... of life. If you discover a fire, operate the nearest alarm. The (**48**) .... officer or his (**49**) .... deputy is responsible for contacting the Fire Brigade.

Evacuation Procedures

The (**50**) .... signal is a series of short pulses of the alarm. When this signal sounds

- switch off all machines
- switch off all (**51**) .... and gas supplies
- shut windows
- evacuate physically (**52**) .... staff

Evacuation Signal

This is a continuous sounding of the alarm. On hearing this signal, everyone should leave by the nearest fire exit.

- walk, don't run
- do not stop to collect (**53**) ....
- do not re-enter the building

(**0**)	RESPONSIBLE
(**47**)	LOSE
(**48**)	SECURE
(**49**)	AUTHORITY
(**50**)	WARN
(**51**)	ELECTRIC
(**52**)	ABLE
(**53**)	BELONG

ADVERTISEMENT

Subscribe Now!

Over a year, a (**54**) .... to our magazine will save you £21 compared with making a monthly purchase at the newsagent's.

There are several methods of (**55**) .... – cheque, credit card or direct debit. Our (**56**) .... costs are much lower if you pay by direct debit, so there is a (**57**) .... of £2 in the price you pay – a total (**58**) .... of £23 over the year. (Please note that this extra discount is not applicable if you pay the special student rate). If you choose this method, you don't have to worry about (**59**) .... because your bank will (**60**) .... transfer the money once a year. We will send you a (**61**) .... a few weeks before it is time to renew. You can cancel at any time and will receive a full refund on any unposted copies.

(**54**)	SUBSCRIBE
(**55**)	PAY
(**56**)	ADMINISTRATE
(**57**)	REDUCE
(**58**)	SAVE
(**59**)	NEW
(**60**)	AUTOMATIC
(**61**)	REMIND

PART 5

PART 5

Tip Strip

Remember:
- highlight the information in the first text that you have to reexpress.

Question 71: Which word will convey the meaning of 'nobody except' in the first text?

Question 73: If they are accessible by car, how do you get there?

Question 74: If the Trust does not provide sheets and towels, what must you do?

For questions **62–74**, read the Historical Cottages Trust Booking Terms leaflet and use the information to complete the numbered gaps in the informal letter. **Use no more than two words** for each gap. The words you need **do not occur** in the leaflet. The exercise begins with an example (**0**).

Example:

0	*in full*		0

Historical Cottages Trust Booking Terms

1 You are required to pay the total price three months before your holiday begins.
2 Payments must be in sterling (internationally recognised credit cards are acceptable).
3 If you cancel within three months of the start of your holiday, you will forfeit the booking fee (unless severe weather prevents you from reaching the property).
4 You must not enter the property before 4 p.m. on the first day and you must not stay longer than 11 a.m. on the last day of your holiday. This is to enable our housekeeper to prepare the property for you and your successors.
5 Dogs are permitted but must be kept off the furniture.
6 Nobody except the people whose names are listed on the booking form must stay in the property. We mind VERY MUCH INDEED about this.
7 Although our properties are in isolated areas, all are easily accessible by car.
8 The cottages are fully equipped but sheets and towels are not provided.

INFORMAL LETTER

Dear Sophie,

I'm enclosing some information about an organisation that rents out interesting old cottages. We stayed in one last year and it was marvellous.

One disadvantage is that you have to pay (**0**) .... three months (**62**) .... Also, they only accept English (**63**) .... but you can use a credit card. Don't book unless you are sure because if you cancel they will not (**64**) .... your money, unless you cancel more than three months before you intend to go, or unless the road to your chosen cottage has become (**65**) .... because of bad weather.

Remember that you have to (**66**) .... after 4 p.m. on the first day and (**67**) .... before 11 a.m. on the last day so that the housekeeper can get the cottage ready for you, and the people who (**68**) .... It will be (**69**) .... for you to take your dogs but don't let them (**70**) .... on the furniture. Remember that the (**71**) .... people who may sleep in the cottage are those whose names are on the booking form. The Trust takes this matter (**72**) ....

You can (**73**) .... to all the properties, so you can take with you whatever you need. You will have to take (**74**) .... sheets and towels in any case.

Love
Jenny

Tip Strip

Remember:

• read your answer carefully, checking grammar and punctuation.

Question 76: Which phrase gives an example of gadgets?

Question 77: Which words often follow 'asked'?

Question 78: What was the purpose of forming the company?

For questions **75–80** read through the following text and then choose from the list **A–J** below the best phrase to fill each of the spaces. Write one letter (**A–J**) in the correct box on your answer sheet. **Some of the suggested answers do not fit at all.** The exercise begins with an example (**0**).

Example: | 0 | *J* | | 0 |

A Telephone Pioneer:
Henry Hunnings (1843–86)

Most people have heard of Alexander Graham Bell, who invented the telephone in 1876. But it was a little-known English priest called Henry Hunnings (**0**) .... . Bell's model could transmit a voice up to about 23km. A year after its invention, Thomas Edison improved on the model by attaching a solid-carbon button inside the mouthpiece. But Hunnings decided to experiment with granular carbon (**75**) .... . This improved the voice clarity and extended the voice-transmission distance to about 72km. Hunnings was granted a patent for his invention in December 1878.

Hunnings was born in 1843 near London. He became a priest in Yorkshire and although much of his time was taken up with Church matters, he had a profound interest in all sorts of gadgets, (**76**) .... . A friend of Hunnings with similar interests, called Cox Walker, built a telephone receiver. In 1880 an American called Anders visited England and asked Walker (**77**) .... . He was impressed and offered Hunnings £1,000 for the patent. The offer was accepted and the Globe Company was formed (**78**) .... . In 1881 Hunnings was granted two patents in the United States for his invention. But by this time so many people and companies were involved in telephone design and manufacture (**79**) .... . There was a famous court case in 1882 when the United Telephone Company took the Globe Company to court for an alleged infringement of its patents. At first it failed to have the Hunnings patent declared invalid (**80**) .... . It then bought the rights to the entire patent from Hunnings.

A   which few people had known about
B   instead of solid carbon
C   but later it partially succeeded
D   except that Hunning's invention was superior
E   in breach of copyright
F   to make telephones in England
G   that conflict resulted
H   particularly those that dealt with magnetism and electricity
I   if he could inspect the Hunnings transmitter

J   who made the first big improvement

Listening (approx. 45 minutes)

Remember:
- read the questions before you listen and try and predict the most likely answers.

Questions 1–3: The key word in the sentence is 'pull'. Listen for this and words which have a similar meaning.

Question 8: In this sentence 'fingers' is the key word, but beware of misleading references that use the same word.

You will hear a short talk about 'Safety in the Home'. For questions **1–10**, fill in the missing information.

You will hear the recording twice.

Safety In The Home

Amanda Brown advises us to take great care with three things that children pull at:

	1
	2
	3

For safety reasons, she suggests that we cover up:

	4
	5

She advises us to lock up or keep out of reach of children:

	6
	7

She advises us to be very careful when we open:

	8

She says that we should tell children not to put their fingers in:

	9

And she is worried about small children trying to operate:

	10

You will hear a message on your answerphone about important changes to the timetable of a conference that you are going to. For questions **11–20**, complete the notes according to the information you hear.

Listen very carefully as you will hear the recording ONCE only.

Conference Arrangements

New time of talk:	11
New place of talk:	12
Accommodation: room number	13
9.30 p.m.: Reception	14
7.15 p.m.: New time of	15
Three things to collect on arrival:	16
	17
	18
Contact number:	19
Phone before:	20

Tip Strip

Question 21: How many things can you think of before you listen? One of them will be mentioned on the tape.

Question 24: What kind of structure does the word 'as' indicate?

Question 27: Can you think of some likely wrong assumptions? You will hear one of them on the tape. Also, think of adjectives that collocate with 'make you...'.

You will hear a radio interview with a doctor, about health and sport. For questions **21–30**, complete each of the statements.

You will hear the recording twice.

Health and Sport

According to Dr Green:

When we start a new sport we should take into account our

	21

If we are under 35, all sports should be

	22

Sports which involve fast and sudden movements should be avoided by people who smoke or who are:

	23

If you restart a sport that you used to do, don't expect to be as		24
Cycling and swimming are safe sports because you can choose		25
Another safe aspect of these sports is that there is support for your		26
Some people wrongly assume that exercise can make them		27
In fact to burn up to 100 grams of fat would take four hours of		28
If we have been exercising, we should not have a sauna or cold shower		29
The most dangerous thing is to exercise when you are		30

You will hear **five** short extracts in which different people talk about accidents they have had.

Accidents

TASK ONE

For questions **31–35**, match the extracts as you hear them with the types of accidents, listed **A–H**.

A   parachuting

B   sailing

C   playing football

D   driving

E   cycling

F   swimming

G   horse riding

H   skiing

	31
	32
	33
	34
	35

TASK TWO

For questions **36–40**, match the extracts as you hear them with the different feelings experienced immediately after the accident by the speakers, listed **A–H**.

A   terror

B   sadness

C   stupidity

D   surprise

E   despair

F   hope

G   resignation

H   anger

	36
	37
	38
	39
	40

Remember that you must complete both tasks as you listen. You will hear the recording twice.

PAPER 5

Speaking (15 minutes)

Tip Strip

Part 1: Remember that in Part 1 the examiner speaks to both candidates and the candidates speak to each other.

Part 2: You don't have to describe the photos in great detail. The important thing is to discuss the topic that the photo illustrates.

Part 3: Remember to look at the other candidate, not at the examiner. Don't speak too quietly – the examiner needs to hear what you are saying.

Part 4: In this part you will be looking at the examiner and also at the other candidate. Always look at the person you are speaking to.

PART 1 (3 minutes)

Answer these questions:

What are you studying now and where?
What are your future plans with regard to your studies?
How will your studies help you to get the job you want?
What changes have taken place in the last few years in the way that students study?

PART 2 (3 or 4 minutes)

Celebration (Describe and comment)

Turn to pictures 1–3 on page 132 which show people celebrating in some way.

Candidate A, describe what they are doing and why you think they are celebrating in this way. You have a minute to do this.

Candidate B, which event would you most like to join in?

Enjoy your meal (Compare, contrast and speculate)

Turn to pictures 1–3 on page 133 which show people eating in different situations.

Candidate B, compare and contrast these situations, saying why you think these people have chosen to eat in that way. You have a minute to do this.

Candidate A, which of these ways of eating most appeals to you?

PART 3 (3 or 4 minutes)

Mobile phones (Discuss, identify and evaluate)

Turn to pictures 1–5 on page 134 which show people using mobile phones. What do you think they are using them for? For which person in the pictures is a mobile phone most useful?

PART 4 (3 or 4 minutes)

Answer these questions:

Did you reach agreement?
How do your opinions differ?
If you have a mobile phone yourself, how do you use it?
What would you use a mobile phone for if you had one?
What, if anything, do you find irritating about the way people use mobile phones?

TEST 3

Reading (1 hour 15 minutes)

PART 1

Tip Strip

Questions 3/4: Look for references to making the most of your skills and to selling yourself.

Question 14: Check what topic you are advised to put last. Then find out how important it is.

Question 15: How many typographical features can you think of before reading the article? Check to see if the words you have thought of actually occur in the text.

Answer questions **1–17** by referring to the newspaper article about curriculum vitaes on page **57**.

Indicate your answers **on the separate answer sheet**.

For questions **1–17**, answer by choosing from the sections of the article (**A–F**).

You may choose any of the sections more than once.

Note: When more than one answer is required, they may be given **in any order**.

Which section

emphasises that your CV must make the reader sit up and pay attention?	**1**	
mentions the usefulness of a CV during the interview?	**2**	
says that self-promotion is absolutely vital?	**3**	**4** ....
emphasises the importance of telling the truth?	**5**	
advises referring to yourself as 'he' or 'she' rather than 'I'?	**6**	
suggests you need a different CV for each job you apply for?	**7**	**8** ....
describes two different types of CV?	**9**	
advises paying attention to the vocabulary you use?	**10**	
suggests that what you did at school may not be important?	**11**	
warns of the consequences of a badly-written CV?	**12**	
emphasises linking your most important abilities to the requirements of the job?	**13**	
states that what you put last is of great importance?	**14**	
mentions typographical features that you can put in your CV?	**15**	
suggests that a CV should not be hand-written?	**16**	
emphasises the importance of your most recent work?	**17**	

Story of your life

A

YOUR curriculum vitae is your most critical selling document. If you get it right it will land you the interviews you want; get it wrong and your hard-earned work experience could be consigned to the waste bin.

As it is the only thing that you can fully control in the job selection process, it is vital that your CV puts across everything you want to say about yourself in the most impressive way. It must highlight your value to the potential employer, as well as leaving the interviewer with a clear reminder of what you could do for them. Not only that, if it gets you on the short list, it will help provide a structure for the interview and encourage your interviewer to focus on your achievements.

B

YOUR aim is to make it as easy as possible for your potential employer to select you, so ensure that your skills, abilities and experience literally shout out from the page. Keep it brief but full of substance, so that they can see at a glance that you would be capable of the job.

Most critical is that you write for the reader. Identify what it is that your potential employer is looking for, so that your CV focuses on their needs. Ideally, you should tailor your CV for each job. Keep sentences short; they are easier to read and have greater impact. Examine each word that you have used to describe yourself to see if a more powerful one could be used. Avoid jargon.

Write your CV in the third person, rather than the first, so that you can give yourself proper credit without appearing brash.

C

KEEP your CV up to date. The interviewer is more interested in what you are doing now and the pertinence of your current skills and experience than in what you were doing ten years ago. Headhunters nowadays advise that your career and corresponding achievements are highlighted up front. So after your name and address and contact number at the top, go straight into details about your employment history, followed by your education and qualifications, finishing with your personal details.

Always put your most recent job first and then work back in chronological order. As people read from left to right, put the most important things on the left side of the page, so state the title of the job you had first, then for whom you did it and finally when you did it. Give a brief description of the scale and scope of the company you worked for. You cannot assume your reader will have heard of it.

Under each particular job you mention, your own achievements are more important than your responsibilities. Quantify and qualify what you actually did in your role, using hard facts to demonstrate the tangible benefits you brought.

D

IF you have been in a career for a long time, you do not need to include your early education and qualifications. Write the information in reverse order and put the qualifications you achieved, then where you achieved them, followed by the date. Include any appropriate training courses you have been on.

Apart from your name, address and contact numbers, which should go at the top of your CV, all other personal details, including your date of birth, marital status and interests should be left to the end.

Interests are an important part of your CV. They can really bring you alive, say something about you as a person, and differentiate you from the rest. Make sure what you put down adds value.

E

HAVING worked on the content, make sure the layout does not let you down. It must look professional and be clear and easy to read. Use headings to help the reader to scan the document and bullet points to focus on key information. Print it on quality paper to ensure a quality impression.

F

IDEALLY, you should customise your CV for each job you are going for, but this may not be practical if you are going for dozens of jobs at a time. What differs fundamentally about the CV you produce is whether it is built around your present job or aimed at a change in your career. CVs appropriate for a change in career will need to pull out relevant transferable skills and this can be done by having a skills and experience section ahead of the career summary. These four to five key skills will match what is on the job specification.

At the end of the day, your CV is all about packaging. If you can't sell yourself, how will you be able to promote the company you are working for? And you must feel comfortable with what you have written, and confident you can back it up.

For questions **18–23**, you must choose which of the paragraphs **A–G** on page **59** fit into the numbered gaps in the following magazine article. There is one extra paragraph which does not fit in any of the gaps.

Indicate your answers **on the separate answer sheet**.

Sleep easy

It's three o'clock in the morning. You're exhausted, but just can't sleep. Relax! Millions like you suffer from sleep problems. Considering how essential sleep is to life, we understand surprisingly little about it. Because we are semi-conscious when we sleep, the whole process is veiled in myth and mystery.

18	

You see, sleeping problems are caused quite simply by modern day living. As we become increasingly out of tune with our bodies and their needs, our primary functions suffer. Insomnia is only one type of sleep disorder. Bad dreams, malsomnia, even snoring if it wakes you – they're all sleep disorders, though mostly short-term and usually related to a sudden change in lifestyle, an imminent event or stress. Trouble really begins when these short-term problems become chronic. So whatever type of sleep disorder you are plagued by, it's time to nip it in the bud.

You're not alone!

19	

What's the problem?
Insomnia literally means sleeplessness and should not be confused with light or erratic sleeping throughout the night. Insomnia falls into two categories, both of which can be short-term or chronic. Some insomniacs can't get to sleep at night. They turn off the light and their mind races, turning thoughts over and over, until they become so desperate to sleep and so afraid of staying awake that their despair prevents them from sleeping, leaving them mentally exhausted by the early hours of the morning. They fall into prolonged deep sleep which deprives them of necessary mental sleep.

20	

Malsomnia means bad sleep, which can also fall into two categories, light sleeping and broken sleeping.

They're not problems in themselves until they begin to affect the sufferers waking hours. Malsomnia, however, is often short-term and directly related to a stressful one-off event.

How to cope
If you have discounted physical causes as the root of your sleeping problems, then it's time to look a little deeper. Your first step is to try not to worry too much. Fear of not sleeping and the consequences of lack of sleep can lead to stress and despair, which then cause insomnia. You are caught in a downward spiral and you have to break the cycle. Don't panic!

21	

Instant self help
Counting sheep may sound a cliché but monotonous or regular mind games can help induce drowsiness. Try listing pleasant things. Try adding up a long list of figures, or counting backwards from 500. Anything to lull your mind to sleep. It can work! Concentrate on the rhythm of your breathing. Sleep with your ear on the pillow, or against your arm and listen to your heart beat.

22	

Although drugs are often the first thing patients reach for when they can't sleep, they have a bad track record when it comes to long-term results, and should only be used if everything else has failed.

Sleep secrets
Don't be misled by your body's lack of movement when you are asleep. Sleep is a period of great rest but also of activity for your body. There are three stages of sleep, and each serves a very different and important function. As you relax, your brain gradually slows down and after about fifteen minutes your brain waves become synchronised. This happens gradually during the transition between wakefulness and sleep. Once you actually drop off to sleep your brain activity continues to slow, until after an hour or ninety minutes you're in a deep sleep. After about an hour and a half of deep sleep you pass into a totally different phase of sleep known as REM (Rapid Eye Movement) sleep.

The brain waves become shorter and faster and your eyes dart around under your closed lids. At the same time your muscles become very relaxed, almost paralysed, and your breathing erratic. This lasts for about ten minutes and is commonly associated with dreaming. When the third stage finishes you go back into a deep sleep stage again. Stages two and three are repeated throughout the night until you wake.

23	

The average person in Europe sleeps around six hours a night – not the traditional eight as you might expect and many doctors are beginning to believe this is quite sufficient to leave you healthy and well-rested. But people often underestimate the amount of sleep they get, simply because the minutes spent lying awake, trying to get to sleep, appear to go slowly.

Sleep problems arise when people ignore their body signals and so develop bad sleeping habits. If someone has a sleepless night but isn't able to sleep during the next day, they are forced to disregard their body's needs and erratic sleep patterns result.

A   Mild exercise like slow walking can help before bedtime, but beware of frantic exercise late at night because it stimulates your heart rate and will keep you awake. Exercise during the day plays a key role in a healthy lifestyle – and good health is essential for sleep. Relaxation techniques can also prepare you for sleep.

B   Slightly less common is the insomniac who falls asleep upon turning out the light, only to awaken again in the early hours of the morning unable to return to sleep until the next evening. Their quality of sleep is fine – they're simply not getting enough.

C   Overeating can cause insomnia and poor sleeping patterns because your digestive system slows down during sleep. It is also worth steering clear of caffeine drinks, such as coffee, tea or cola, late at night as they can stimulate your brain and keep you awake. Milky drinks are the traditional bedtime companions of the troubled sleeper.

D   It is now known that REM sleep serves a different function to deep sleep. Deep sleep restores the body, allowing growth hormones and antibodies to be released into the blood to repair cells. REM sleep rests the mind, allowing it to sort through the day's activities and experiences in order to 'file' them for future reference. Deprivation of either of these will have different effects for the sufferer. One will leave you physically exhausted, the other mentally.

E   Almost everyone suffers from some sort of sleep disorder at some time in their lives. But for some the suffering goes on and on. You can't always spot the typical insomniacs. They don't yawn constantly, have red-rimmed eyes, or fall asleep at their desks. Neither are they invariably creative geniuses. Sleep disorder sufferers are a silent majority – everyday people with a chronic problem.

F   Start by hiding your alarm clock from view. If you don't know the time, you won't worry about it. Read a relaxing book, or perhaps try listening to a relaxation tape before turning out the light. During the daytime, try to analyse your life to find a cause for your sleeplessness. It helps to ask yourself a few basic questions like: 'Am I happy / satisfied?', 'Can I cope?', 'What will make me happy / satisfied?' Most chronic insomniacs are chronic avoiders of problems. So try to face up to and solve your worries – otherwise anxieties you have during the day will follow you to bed at night.

G   Sleeping disorders have reached epidemic proportions in the Western World. Only now are sleep scientists beginning to look more closely at the problem, not to find a cure but to eradicate the causes. And they're discovering that it's not so much the quantity but the quality of sleep that counts. This could explain the success of certain famous light sleepers.

Tip Strip

Question 18: Which paragraph contrasts with 'myth and mystery' by suggesting that more things will be discovered?

Question 21: The paragraph before says 'try not to worry too much'. Which other paragraph mentions worries and anxieties?

Question 22: Which paragraph mentions activities that contrast with counting, breathing and taking drugs?

Question 23: Which paragraph refers to eye movement in a different way?

Read the following newspaper article and then answer questions **24–30** on page **61**. On your answer sheet, indicate the letter **A**, **B**, **C** or **D** against the number of each question, **24–30**. Give only one answer to each question.

Indicate your answers **on the separate answer sheet**.

Still Sprinting

Derek Parker talks to the millionaire author Jeffrey Archer.

DESPITE the recent and expensive failure of his latest West End* play, Jeffrey Archer is not noticeably down and a considerable distance from out. With *Kane and Abel* having sold over three million copies in England and the paperback of *Not a Penny More, Not a Penny Less* continuing to nip smartly out of the bookshops at the rate of a thousand copies a day, fifteen years after its first publication, he has little real reason to be permanently dispirited.

It's common knowledge that literature is not his first love. He only started writing in his mid-thirties, when a promising political career collapsed and he resigned a safe seat in Parliament amid business and financial difficulties which would have crushed most men for good. The legend that he wrote his first novel with the cold-blooded intention of making a fortune, is, however, only a legend.

'I always tell people who say that, and who aren't in the profession, that if it were true – and if it were that easy – everyone'd be doing it. No, I did it much more as an exorcism, to keep working after I'd left the House, because I couldn't get a job. It was vitally important to be physically working – to believe in the work ethic. Oh yes, I wanted the book to be published, to be read, but it was much more to have done something. In fact, the advance on the first book was £3000, and they published 3000 copies, so you couldn't say I wrote it for the money.'

Penny became an international best seller, and from that day, as an author, he has never looked back.

Both as a reader and author, Archer divides novelists into storytellers and writers. Certainly with him, the important thing is the story. This doesn't come easy.

'In fact very little comes, to begin with. I'm writing a book currently – I've done the first draft. But I never know what's on the next line, what's in the next paragraph, what's on the next page. I just let it happen.'

It happens mainly between six and eight in the morning. 'I like that session. It's the only original session. Then I correct from three till five, correct from six till eight, go to bed at nine o'clock. Two thousand words if it's a good day.'

The writing has to fit into a political schedule. Still offered several safe Parliamentary seats a year, which he firmly turns down, he accepts innumerable speaking engagements all over the country. But at certain times of the year 'nobody wants you. I went away on December 15th to write until January 15th. There are ten weeks a year when nobody wants you to speak, and that's when the writing gets done.'

He values his relationship with his publisher to an extent which must warm their hearts. 'I don't think authors can have natural friends in publishing houses; but there's mutual respect. They're good publishers, and I'm proud to be with them.'

And his editor?

'My editor is called Richard Cohen. He's tough. He drives me and drives me. He never writes a word – that's not his job; but he guides, guides, guides the whole time – he's never satisfied. He doesn't have a lot to do with plot – I believe he thinks that's my strength. He'll get me to build characters – build, build, build, the whole time. He knows he's right. He'll go on and on at me; he won't give in. Kicking him has absolutely no effect – he doesn't even bruise. Nine times out of ten, I believe he's right. He has tremendous judgement. He's a class editor.'

Influences?

'I like story-tellers. I'm a story-teller; I'm not good enough to be a writer. I'm Jeffrey Archer and I tell a tale, I hope people turn the pages, and I hope they enjoy it, and in the end, that's what I ask for'. ∎

*West End: the area of London where many major theatres are found.

24 What was Jeffrey Archer's reaction to the failure of his play?

    A   He was thoroughly put out.
    B   He regretted the wasted effort.
    C   He was sorry about the amount of money he lost.
    D   He was unaffected by it.

25 What is Jeffrey Archer's main interest in life?

    A   writing
    B   politics
    C   business
    D   theatre

26 Why did he write his first novel?

    A   To show how good a story-teller he could be.
    B   To have some work to do.
    C   To make money.
    D   To prove he was successful at something.

27 When he's writing, Jeffrey Archer

    A   has no difficulty thinking up a story.
    B   finds the actual writing easy.
    C   maps out an overall plan of the book first.
    D   has a fixed routine.

28 Apart from writing novels what else does Jeffrey Archer do?

    A   He stands for election to Parliament.
    B   He makes a lot of speeches.
    C   He does other kinds of writing.
    D   He takes long holidays.

29 What is his attitude to his publishers?

    A   He regards them as friends.
    B   He respects their work.
    C   He considers them to be the best in the profession.
    D   He feels he has to flatter them.

30 What is his relationship with his editor like?

    A   They continually argue.
    B   They disagree about priorities.
    C   The editor gives advice about the storyline.
    D   The editor stresses the importance of the characters.

Tip Strip

Question 25: All these activities are mentioned but which one is mentioned several times, in different places in the text, and in several different ways?

Question 27: For this question, look for evidence that three of the options are actually incorrect. For example, A is wrong, the text says that he does find it difficult to think up a story.

PART 4

Answer questions **31–48** by referring to the newspaper article about spas on pages **63–64**.

Indicate your answers **on the separate answer sheet**.

For questions **31–48**, answer by choosing from the list (**A–D**) on the right below.

Some choices may be required more than once.

Note: When more than one answer is required, these may be given **in any order**.

the location smells unpleasant	31	
ingredients from this spa are used in beauty products	32	
in the past this spa was popular with the wealthy	33	
the treatment consists of bathing in mud mixed with water	34	
does not benefit from an immediately attractive setting	35	
offers unsophisticated accommodation	36 .... 37	
users should take care not to get burnt by hot water	38	
those taking the treatment here wear special clothing on the way to the treatment site	39	**A** Vichy
provides treatment for patients funded by the state	40	**B** Vulcano
a boat trip is necessary to get there	41	**C** Neydharting
for the treatment to be effective, a coating must be left on the skin for a specified period	42	**D** Blue Lagoon
it has types of water that make it different from all other spas	43	
people enter a building to obtain drinking water	44	
this spa is in a completely undeveloped state	45 .... 46	
it could be an extremely dangerous place	47	
this spa was popular several hundred years ago	48	

Springing Hot from the Bowels of the Earth

The ancient custom of taking the waters for the sake of health, beauty and pleasure is flourishing as never before. June Sampson surveys the world of spas from Iceland to Sicily.

Vichy washes away past cares

It was Napoleon III who put Vichy on the map. He believed in the remarkable restorative powers of the local springs and under his patronage Vichy became famous as the Queen of Spas. The atmosphere of imperial glamour survives among the promenades, opera house, casino and 526 hectares of parks and gardens which once lured the richest and most fashionable of 19th century Europe. However, the first sight to strike the visitor is a steady stream of people carrying little wicker containers and heading as one, to the Hall des Sources. The elegant conservatory-like building is home to what dedicated Vichy pilgrims regard as the fount of life. Amid the flowers, pillars and palm trees are rows of taps dispensing the various mineral waters and it is this menu of different waters from twelve springs which makes the spa unique.

When you land on the rocky shore, you are greeted by a horrible stench. This is from the sulphides seeping from the volcano in bilious clouds which stain the craggy moonscape fantastic shades of pink, yellow and green. The sulphur collects in an outcrop near the beach. The concentrated sulphur products are an excellent natural beauty treatment. There is no cure centre or facilities – the pool is simply open to everyone. The effect is like sitting in a large natural Jacuzzi, but the experience is not quite as serene as it looks, for scalding water bubbling through the rock can catch out the unwary. Even those who take a dip in the sea to cool off can find themselves suddenly blasted by a boiling jet. But once you have found a spot where the water is a relaxing bath temperature, you lie back and contemplate the active volcano, towering above the scene, with steam issuing from the fissures in its sides.

Poaching under the volcano

One of the chief attractions of a spa holiday is the escape from the stresses of life, and nowhere offers more perfect solitude than Vulcano, the southern-most of the Aeolian islands off the north coast of Sicily. Vulcano's natural resources have remained miraculously untapped by tourism. Most visitors are day trippers who come by hydrofoil from Lipari, the chief island of the Aeolian group.

Mud, glorious mud

Wallowing in a muddy bog hours from anywhere might seem a curious way to spend a holiday. However, this unique spa is renowned for the miraculous powers of its baths and treatments. The secret lies in the Moor, a dark, oozing mud found only at Neydharting, a strange area of moorland set amid lakes and gentle green hills. The Romans were aware of its healing properties and it was a fashionable spa centre in medieval times – a fact confirmed by the recent unearthing of the remains of medieval wooden baths. Gradually, however, the baths went out of fashion and farmers began to drain the land, so destroying large tracts of the Moor. Today it survives only in one isolated corner of the valley, from which it is pumped to the spa centre by carefully concealed pipes.

At the spa, the emphasis is on simplicity, with plain functional accommodation just a few paces away from the treatment centre. The focal point of each day is the Moor bath. It is a surprisingly pleasurable experience. A bath of water is run at 37°C and mixed with a prescribed dosage of Moor until it resembles a rich soup, in which you soak luxuriously. After half an hour you are eased tenderly out of the bath, and, still wet and muddy, swaddled in cotton sheets and left in a state of drowsy euphoria to rest for an hour. A film of Moor has built up over 30,000 years from medicinal herbs and plants which, steeped in the hard water of the area, have broken down to yield a potent cocktail of potentially therapeutic substances. Certainly the German and Australian medical establishments have enough faith in Moor's healing powers for them to send their patients to Neydharting at the expense of the public health services. Others come to use the mud for cosmetic purposes and it has now been incorporated in a range of beauty products. A variety of walks takes the place of the more sophisticated pursuits available in many spa towns.

Where hell boils beneath your feet

The chunks of lava piled up outside the window like broken tarmac, rising to meet the power station beyond which billowed clouds of effluence into the grey sky. Thordur Stafansson, owner of the Blue Lagoon motel in Iceland, exclaimed: 'I can feel hell boiling under our feet.' Never mind under our feet, we could see it all around. And it got worse. We were expected to swim in the waste product vomited out by a mass of pipes and steel. Swathed in white robes with pointed hoods, we wandered through the lava fields towards the lagoon. The mind grappled for suitable similes. Whatever it was, it certainly didn't seem to belong to Planet Earth.

By the time we lowered our bodies into the waters we had given up wondering what would happen next. Much to our surprise it felt wonderful. The hot salt water, warmed by the earth's core gave off tendrils of steam that created a surreal atmosphere. Hot water flooded over us, followed by cool water – giving the unusual impression that the water was somehow textured. Psoriasis sufferers claim to find relief from their painful, disfiguring skin complaint through regular immersions in the lagoon.

If you are lucky enough not to need a long treatment, there is little to keep you here for more than a few days. The Blue Lagoon is a motel rather than the spa it has ambitions to become. While some may be put off by the lack of facilities, others may find a raw appeal about the place. Once you venture into the island's interior, the glorious virgin beauty of this remote place quickly becomes obvious. There is evidence everywhere of geological activity. Iceland is both benevolent and hostile – it provides central heating and Blue Lagoons, but could also swallow you up in lava or hostile seas. Its people show both resignation and acceptance, which goes some way to explain how they could think of creating a health spa right beside a factory.

PART 1

Tip Strip

Question 1: Use a report layout and a formal register.
Use words to describe the percentages in the questionnaire, e.g. 'the majority of students', 'half the students', 'a few students', etc.
Remember to paraphrase the comments. Don't use exactly the same words.
Remember to respond to the Principal's suggestion for a meeting.

1 You have recently carried out a survey to find out what students think of the restaurant in the college where you are studying.

Read the results of the questionnaire below, and the written comments and note sent to you by the principal. Then, **using the information carefully**, write a report for the principal, saying what you discovered and making recommendations.

Write approximately 250 words. You should use your own words as far as possible.

Questionnaire

Students' opinions of the restaurant
(100 questionnaires distributed, 80 returned)

	VERY GOOD	SATISFACTORY	UNSATISFACTORY
QUALITY OF FOOD	10	70	0
STANDARD OF COOKING	20	50	10
VARIETY OF FOOD	0	10	70
OPENING HOURS	10	60	10
COMFORT	0	20	60
PRICES	60	20	0
CLEANLINESS	20	50	10
COURTESY OF STAFF	20	50	10

Comments from students

Same menu every week. If it's curry, it must be Friday. It never changes.

No proper vegetarian food – only salads. Coffee is appalling – why not a proper coffee-making machine instead of just instant coffee?

The cook does his best - but he only seems to know seven recipes.
It's cheap but we'd pay more for better.

Could be open longer hours. Don't finish drama class until 1.30 and restaurant closes at 2.00.

On busy days there's never enough tables.

Note from Principal

```
If your report is ready by Friday, I will be able to call a meeting
within two weeks to discuss its contents.
```

Choose **one** of the following writing tasks. Your answer should follow exactly the instructions given. Write approximately 250 words.

Tip Strip

Question 2: Make sure your leaflet has an eye-catching heading. Use subheadings suggested by the question, e.g. 'What we need', 'Who are we helping?', etc.

Question 3: Your letter needs 3–5 paragraphs. You should combine a sympathetic response with practical suggestions.

Question 4: Note that the phrases 'such things as' means that you can include other things which are not mentioned, providing they are relevant to young people. Remember that you are writing the actual brochure – do not include references to complaints about official tourist literature.

Question 5: You need 3–5 paragraphs. Address the letter to your boss by name, for example, 'Dear Mr Brown', and end 'Yours sincerely'. Make it clear that you wish to return to work at the end of your year off. Be precise about dates.

2 As Student Union Officer you are going to organise a sale of goods to raise money for a charity. You want friends and relatives to give you things which they no longer need, or things that they have made. Write a leaflet saying what sort of things you want for the sale, which charity it is for, why you have chosen that charity and how and when the goods will be collected or delivered.

Write the **leaflet**.

3 A British friend of yours has just started living and working in a town in your country, but not the one where you live. He / she has written to you saying that he / she has not been able to make any new friends and is feeling lonely. Write to your friend, making some helpful suggestions.

Write your **letter**.

4 The town where you live receives many visits from groups of young people from other countries. They complain that the official tourist literature about the town does not tell them what they want to know. You have been asked to write a brochure which gives information about such things as transport, food and drink and entertainment, but in a way that is relevant and interesting to young people aged 16–25.

Write the **brochure**.

5 You have been working for the same company for several years in an enjoyable, interesting and well-paid job. Your boss has a high opinion of you. However, you have decided that you would like to have a year off (without pay) to travel and study. Write a letter to your boss explaining why you would like to have this year off, what you intend to do and how the company would benefit when you return to work.

Write your **letter**.

PAPER 3   English in Use (1 hour 30 minutes)

PART 1

Tip Strip

Question 2: This is a fixed phrase – prevention is better than ...

Question 6: Which word makes a contrast with the complex electronic systems already mentioned?

Question 15: This refers to the police finding stolen goods. Which word best expresses this idea?

For questions **1–15**, read the text below and then decide which word best fits each space. Put the letter you choose for each question in the correct box on your answer sheet. The exercise begins with an example (**0**).

Example:

0	*A*		0

SHOPLIFTING

Last year, losses from shops through shoplifting and theft by staff (**0**) .... to over £1 billion. There are many (**1**) .... for shopkeepers themselves to reduce shoplifting. As with all types of crime, prevention is better than (**2**) .... . The best deterrent is the (**3**) .... of staff properly trained in how to identify potential shoplifters. There are also many security (**4**) .... now available. Video camera surveillance is a popular system, even with quite small retailers. In clothes shops, magnetic tag marking systems that set off an alarm have proved their (**5**) .... . However, there are many (**6**) .... measures that retailers should consider. Better lighting and ceiling-hung mirrors can help staff to (**7**) .... all parts of the display area. Similarly, simply arranging shelves and display units to allow clear (**8**) .... of vision is a good deterrent.

Another problem for retailers is the (**9**) .... of stolen credit cards to buy goods and services. Many retailers avoid this by always checking the (**10**) .... of a card used for purchase. Electronic systems are now available to (**11**) .... up the procedure.

Most companies keep a petty (**12**) .... box for small expenses. They are a popular (**13**) .... for thieves. It is not enough to have a box that locks. A thief can steal it and then open it at leisure. Lock it in a drawer as well. Telephones, typewriters, word processors and computers are also vulnerable because they are (**14**) .... . Property marking is a good deterrent and helps the police return stolen goods if they are (**15**) .... . And remember that in many businesses information is valuable to competitors and should be protected.

	A		B		C		D	
0	(A) amounted		B accumulated		C went		D added	
1	(A) opportunities		B schemes		C ideas		D occasions	✗
2	A remedy		B loss		C cure		D conviction	✓
3	A knowledge		B presence		C number		D importance	✓
4	A devices		B methods		C tricks		D machines	✓
5	A reliability		(B) worth		C valuation		D identity	✗
6	A better		B easier		C simpler		D bigger	✓
7	A notice		B watch		C control		D regard	✓
8	(A) fields		B areas		C systems		D angles	✗
9	A employment		B application		C technique		D use	✓
10	A honesty		B forgery		C validity		D value	✓
11	A speed		B check		C take		D key	✓
12	A money		B bank		C saving		D cash	✓
13	A robbery		(B) target		C aim		D object	✗
14	(A) portable		B expensive		C stolen		D attractive	✗
15	A reported		B known		C revealed		(D) traced	✗

Tip Strip

Question 17: You need a word that is part of a phrase meaning 'for example'.

Question 18: What is another phrase for 'a large amount'?

Question 22: Will glass definitely snap or only probably snap?

Question 24: 'Breaking' is a gerund, so you need a preposition here.

Question 25: Which word is a substitute for 'it' in the middle of a sentence?

Question 29: What comes next gives you the reason why steel is used.

For questions **16–30** complete the following article by writing each missing word in the correct box on your answer sheet. **Use only one word for each space.** The exercise begins with an example (**0**).

Example: | 0 | *most* | 0 |

Across the Gap

Some of the (**0**) .... impressive structures in the world are bridges. Bridges have to be built to withstand a variety of forces. These forces come (**16**) .... a combination of factors: the weight of the bridge, the weight of the traffic, and the strains exerted by the weather, (**17**) .... as wind, rain and snow. Bridges are costly to build and engineers go to a great (**18**) .... of trouble to ensure that they are safe, yet use the minimum amount of material. To be (**19**) .... to do this they must fully understand the properties of the materials they are going to use. (**20**) .... materials, for example, are easy to bend. They are flexible. Flexible materials can be useful in bridge-building (**21**) .... need to be combined with stiffer materials to support large loads. Stiff materials are difficult to bend but tend to be brittle. Glass, for instance, is a stiff material but (**22**) .... snap easily if you try to bend it. Stiff materials can be very hard to compress and are useful (**23**) .... used as supporting pillars in bridges.

The property that is perhaps the most important in bridge-building materials is the strength to withstand large forces (**24**) .... breaking. Steel is such a strong material (**25**) .... is why it is often used. Concrete is a stiff material and, (**26**) .... glass, tends to snap if bending forces are applied, but it is very strong when compressed. If concrete is used (**27**) .... support a bending force then it must be reinforced with (**28**) .... material. Steel is usually used (**29**) .... it is relatively cheap and is good (**30**) .... supporting bending forces.

Tip Strip

Line 32: In this line, is 'love' a verb or a noun?

Line 34: What is the subject of the verb 'is'?

Line 40: Is this a general statement or about a specific group? How are men referred to in line 41?

In **most** lines of the following text there is **one** unnecessary word. It is either grammatically inncorrect or does not fit in with the sense of the text. For each numbered line **31–46** find this word and then write it in the box on your answer sheet. Some lines are correct. Indicate these lines with a tick (✓) in the box. The exercise begins with two examples (**0**).

Examples:

0	✓	0
00	*proven*	0

Are Women More Romantic Than Men?

0 .... It's a subject that will probably be debated until the end of time, but

00 .... on the evidence proven available to date psychologists tend to feel

31 .... just that women do not fall in love as readily as men do.

32 .... Moreover, women seem to fall out of they love more quickly and suffer

33 .... less of long-term distress than men do when a relationship breaks up.

34 .... Why this should be so it is also a controversial question about which

35 .... psychologists have differing opinions. One view contends that in

36 .... cultures where a woman is allowed how to choose a mate, as opposed to

37 .... the family organised arranging a marriage, the woman must look out for

38 .... her own best interests. She seeks the man who is best be able to

39 .... provide for her and their future children. Some psychologists think

40 .... that this may explain why it is not uncommon for the women to be

41 .... attracted to regard men with power – physical, financial or social. Men,

42 .... by contrast, are prone to fall in love themselves very quickly and be

43 .... much less critical than women of the qualities of the person they

44 .... love. According to one study, men are so far more likely than women to

45 .... believe in 'love at the first sight' and that 'true love comes along

46 .... just once in life'. Seventy per cent of men said they believed these things.

Tip Strip

Question 49: Is this singular or plural?

Question 56: Which word from 'economy' means 'inexpensive'?

Question 61: Is the meaning positive or negative?

For questions **47–61** read the two texts below. Use the words in the boxes to form one word that fits in the same numbered space in the text. Write the new word in the correct box on your answer sheet. The exercise begins with an example (**0**).

Example:

0	*extensive*		0
			☐ ▨

A REVIEW

Tudor House

This restaurant was opened just two weeks ago after an (**0**) .... and detailed programme of (**47**) .... and renovation of one of the oldest buildings in town. The exact age of the building was (**48**) .... until foundations were discovered which date back to the fifteenth century. At one point the building work was halted so that (**49**) .... could carry out excavations. Some of the interesting (**50**) .... they made are now on display in the restaurant.

There has been a beautiful and effective (**51**) .... of the traditional building and the modern restaurant. It has a charming and (**52**) .... atmosphere where customers can relax and enjoy their meals. An additional (**53**) .... is the large garden which has room for fifty customers to enjoy al fresco eating in the summer months.

(0)	EXTEND
(47)	RESTORE
(48)	KNOW
(49)	ARCHAEOLOGY
(50)	DISCOVER
(51)	INTEGRATE
(52)	ROMANCE
(53)	ATTRACT

A LEAFLET

A New Way To Get To The Airport

The official (**54**) .... of the new Airport Express took place only yesterday but it has been in full (**55**) .... for the past three weeks. This new train service takes you from the centre of the city to the airport very rapidly (only twenty minutes) and at a very (**56**) .... price (only £5 one-way). The carriages are comfortable and (**57**) .... but no food and drink is available because the journey is so short. There are, however, uniformed (**58**) .... who will provide passengers with help and advice. There is an on-board television service with information about (**59**) .... and airport facilities or, on the journey from the airport, hotels and train services. In addition, the train has telephones for passengers to use. Many travellers are already choosing the train in (**60**) .... to a long, (**61**) .... and tiring journey by car or taxi.

(54)	OPEN
(55)	OPERATE
(56)	ECONOMY
(57)	SPACE
(58)	ATTEND
(59)	FLY
(60)	PREFER
(61)	PLEASE

Tip Strip

Question 62: What is another word for 14 days?

Question 63: If you are a beginner, what don't you have?

Question 70: If there is 'no charge' the course must be ... what?

For questions **62–74**, read the following formal notice and use the information to complete the numbered gaps in the informal letter. Then write the new words in the correct spaces on your answer sheet. **Use no more than two words** for each gap. Words you need **do not occur** in the notice. The exercise begins with an example (**0**).

Example:

0	*working for*

0
☐ ▆

Staff In-Service Training Scheme

14-day Adventure Course in North Wales
Activities include: mountaineering, caving, canoeing, abseiling, scuba-diving.

- **Suitable for complete beginners – full training given.**
- **Emphasis on developing leadership skills.**
- **All equipment provided but you must bring your own boots.**

Places are very limited. Apply before January 31st. Application forms are available at Reception. Staff who attended this course in March cannot re-apply.

There is no charge for this course.

Attending this course will improve the chances of employees who are thinking of applying for promotion within the company. Staff who reach an adequate standard on the course will receive a certificate. The company will receive a full report on the physical and mental qualities that staff have shown during the course, including their ability to work under pressure and motivate others to achieve goals. The course must be taken as part of your annual leave entitlement.

INFORMAL LETTER

---

26 January 20––

Dear Caroline,

Since you have been away this week at the sales conference, I thought I should write to you about another course the company is offering. It's only for people who are already (**0**) .... the company. It's a course in North Wales which lasts a (**62**) .... and includes a lot of adventurous activities. You don't need any (**63**) .... because you can learn things from scratch. Everything you need for the activities is provided (**64**) .... boots. There are only (**65**) .... places and you must apply before (**66**) .... of this month. You haven't (**67**) ...., have you? There was one (**68**) .... year and staff who went on that can't (**69**) ....

With this letter I have enclosed an application form for you to fill in and return. The course is completely (**70**) .... (which is good, isn't it? I think it normally costs about £800). It seems that attending this course will be an (**71**) .... for anyone hoping to be promoted. You also get a certificate if you are (**72**) .... and the company is told (**73**) .... you did on the course. Unfortunately, going on the course means (**74**) .... two weeks of your holiday. Do you think it is worth it?

Best wishes,
Camilla

Tip Strip

Question 75: The word 'estimating' strongly suggests that a reference to a number will come next.

Question 77: Because of the word 'surprise' what comes next must refer to weather which is completely different from tropical weather.

Question 80: The word 'amazingly' suggests that what comes next is an extreme and astonishing piece of information.

For questions **75–80** read through the following text and then choose from the list **A–J** below the best phrase to fill each of the spaces. Write one letter (**A–J**) in the correct box on your answer sheet. **Some of the suggested answers do not fit at all.** The exercise begins with an example (**0**).

Example: | **0** | *g* | | **0** |
|---|---|---|---|

Why You Feel Under the Weather

MOST of us casually tune in to the weather forecast to find out whether we should take an umbrella to work, or if we should go to the football match. But perhaps we should listen more carefully, because the day's weather could seriously affect how we feel. Of course, we mostly feel good when the sun shines and subdued when it rains. But scientists and doctors are starting to realise (**0**) .... . Growing numbers of people are being diagnosed as weather-sensitive, with some experts estimating (**75**) .... .

The hazards of hot climates are well known. When we head for holidays in the tropics we know (**76**) .... . It comes as a surprise to learn (**77**) .... . Weather-related symptoms can be far more severe than those we traditionally associate with inclement weather, such as headaches and muscular pain. Of course, sufferers from rheumatism have long complained (**78**) .... . More dangerously a cold snap can bring on fatal heart attacks and strokes in the elderly. In Britain there are far more deaths a week in the winter than in the summer. It is generally accepted (**79**) .... . Asthma, allergies and some psychological conditions are all markedly affected by changes in the weather. The most dramatic cases occur on warm dry days when the sky is filled with low clouds. In these conditions some people go from excellent health to marked illness in a matter of minutes. And amazingly, a few people are so acutely weather-sensitive (**80**) .... .

A that they completely lose consciousness during thunder and lightning storms
B that there is no evidence for these ideas
C that low temperatures are a causative factor in many cases
D that they cannot expose themselves to sunlight
E that one third of the population could be adversely affected
F that they feel worse when it rains
G that we must protect ourselves against the harmful rays of the sun
H that even temperate climates present a health risk
I that these diseases are no longer dangerous

J that cold weather can bring not just low temperatures but also depression and anxiety

PART 1

Tip Strip

Question 1: When do you think electric cars were first used?

Question 3: What are the two different and incompatible things electric cars can do?

You will hear someone talking about electric cars, past and present. Listen to the recording and for questions **1–10**, complete the missing information.

You will hear the recording twice.

Electric Cars

Contrary to popular belief, electric cars existed in the

	1

At one time, in comparison with petrol-driven cars, electric cars were

	2

Designers of electric cars must choose between		**3**

Jenatzy's cars went very fast but not		**4**

A big advantage of electric cars is that they do not		**5**

LA405: This car has two		**6**

The energy for air-conditioning comes from the

	7

It can be recharged while the driver is at work or

	8

Impulse: Unlike the LA405, its power source is		**9**

Compared with petrol-driven cars, it performs		**10**

Tip Strip

Question 12: Which parts of the address are probably missing? Listen carefully for these.

Question 17: What possible problems could occur with an order? Try and predict the possibilities before you listen.

Question 20: What type of information will come after 'within...'?

You will hear a message left by a customer on a telephone answering machine at the office of Zenith Computer Software Supplies Ltd. Look at the form below and fill in the information for questions **11–20**.

Listen very carefully as you will hear the recording ONCE only.

A Dissatisfied Customer

Zenith Computer Software Supplies Ltd
Ansaphone Message

From

Name: | **11** | *John Smith*

Address: | **12** | *Marsham, Gloucestershire*

Contact number: | **13**

Item concerned: *Stand Alone Modem*

Model number: | **14**

Date of order: | **15**

Customer code: | **16**

Nature of problem: *Order* | **17**

Previous contact: *Yes, spoke to* | **18**
a week ago

Name of part: | **19** | *DC 10 5 V*

Degree of urgency? *Customer must have part within*

| **20**

Tip Strip

Question 26: A drawback is a disadvantage, so you are listening for a negative point.

Question 27: In this context 'post' means a job, so you are listening for references to different types of job.

Question 30: After the words 'afraid of' you need to write a word ending in '-ing'.

You will hear a radio programme in which three people discuss the uses of graphology. For questions **21–30**, complete the information using an appropriate word or short phrase.

You will hear the recording twice.

The Uses of Graphology

Tom Phelps's book is called [   ] **21**

Margot Sayer's particular interest is [   ] **22**

What three personality traits does Tom say he can assess from handwriting?

[   ] **23**

[   ] **24**

[   ] **25**

What drawback does Tom refer to when companies use graphologists?

[   ] **26**

For what type of post is graphology used?

[   ] **27**

What traditional thing does Margot criticise?

[   ] **28**

Margot says the research evidence in favour of graphology is

[   ] **29**

Tom thinks pyschologists are opposed to graphologists because they are afraid of

[   ] **30**

You will hear **five** short extracts in which different people comment on their experiences of being prizewinners. For questions **31–40**, choose the correct option **A**, **B** or **C**. You will hear the recording twice.

Tip Strip

Question 31: Did a performance of a play take place?

Question 34: What is the meaning of the expression 'the real carrot'?

Question 37: The speaker mentions a contract and further study but how are they related to the prize?

The Prizewinners

31 In order to win the prize, the first speaker had to
   A learn something by heart.
   B give a speech.
   C act in a play.

32 The first speaker knew he had won
   A when the principal phoned him.
   B because he was offered a job.
   C some time after the performance.

33 The second speaker entered the competition because
   A she wanted to win money.
   B she thought it would lead to more work.
   C she is keen on art exhibitions.

34 The painting the speaker entered for the competition was
   A a still life painting of vegetables.
   B an extremely large painting.
   C not what she really wanted to paint.

35 When she took part in the competition, the third speaker
   A was much more interested in other things.
   B gave a very popular performance.
   C always felt happy and relaxed.

36 After winning, the third speaker
   A did not change her plans.
   B decided to go to university.
   C worked abroad.

37 As part of the prize, the fourth speaker
   A signed an important contract.
   B was able to do a course of study.
   C travelled to New York.

38 As a result of winning, the fourth speaker
   A was offered a teaching post.
   B was able to join a ballet company.
   C realised he had little prospect of success in his career.

39 What happened when the fifth speaker went to college?
   A He continued to excel in athletics.
   B He discovered a new talent.
   C He found it rather disappointing.

40 How does the fifth speaker now feel about winning?
   A He has some regrets.
   B It was the best time of his life.
   C He thinks it led to wrong decisions.

PAPER 5   Speaking (15 minutes)

PART 1   (3 minutes)

Answer these questions:

Where are you living now and do you like the place you are living in?
How does it compare with places that you have lived in before?
What plans do you have to live in a different place in the future?
What would be your ideal place to live?

PART 2   (3 or 4 minutes)

A Place To Live (Describe, compare and speculate)

Turn to pictures 1–4 on page 135 which show four different rooms in houses or flats.

Candidate A, describe and compare these rooms and say what you think the person who lives there would be like. You have a minute to do this.

Candidate B, which room would you most like to live in?

Pollution (Describe, compare and speculate)

Turn to pictures 1–4 on page 136 which show examples of pollution.

Candidate B, compare and contrast these situations, saying what the possible effects might be. You have a minute to do this.

Candidate A, which seems to you to be the worst example of pollution and why?

PART 3   (3 or 4 minutes)

Magazine Covers (Discuss, speculate and select)

Turn to pictures 1–5 on page 137 which show possible covers for a new magazine about astronomy and space exploration, intended for young people aged 13–20.

Which cover do you think would be the most effective in attracting interest and why?

PART 4   (3 or 4 minutes)

Answer these questions:

Did you reach agreement?
How do your opinions differ?
What, if anything, do you find interesting about this topic?
What kind of things would you expect to read in such a magazine?

TEST 4

PAPER 1   **Reading** (1 hour 15 minutes)

PART 1

Answer questions **1–16** by referring to the newspaper article on page **79**.

Indicate your answers **on the separate answer sheet**.

For questions **1–16**, answer by choosing from the list (**A–F**) on the right below.

Some choices may be required more than once.

Which person

works for a literary agent?   **1** ....

made an offer to a young author?   **2** ....

did not expect the approval of publishers?   **3** ....

appreciates the work of teachers on the
course?   **4** ....

criticises other universities without naming
them?   **5** ....

declined to reveal some writers' names?   **6** ....

explains the publishers' point of view?   **7** ....

experienced some good fortune?   **8** ....

did not have a good opinion of creative
writing courses?   **9** ....

found parts of the course rather frightening?   **10** ....

is not sure that the ability to write novels can
be taught?   **11** ....

appreciated the comments of students on
the course?   **12** ....

has done some writing but not yet written
a novel?   **13** ....

has written more than one novel?   **14** ....

emphasises the practical nature of the course?   **15** ....

has written a novel that has not yet been
published?   **16** ....

A Emma Lee-Potter

B Richard Francis

C Michael Schmidt

D Anna Davis

E Lee Braxton

F Clare Wigfall

WRITING ON THE WALL

THE first acknowledgement inside Emma Lee-Potter's debut novel *Hard Copy*, published this month by Piatkus is to Richard Francis and Michael Schmidt, 'Without whom I would have never started writing'. Francis and Schmidt were her tutors on a two-year taught MA in novel writing at the University of Manchester.

Emma Lee-Potter is not the first of Francis and Schmidt's students to sign a publishing deal. Since the programme started five years ago, five have already found a commercial outlet for their work – four others also have their work under consideration at agents and publishers. Many of them are starting with reworked versions of their MA thesis – practical vindications of a course that was greeted with disdain by many lecturers, who maintained that creative writing was not academically valid and you could not – and should not – teach people to write fiction.

'For many years,' says Francis, 'I was suspicious of creative writing programmes. I spent a large part of my career as an academic who wrote novels, but I never really connected the two activities very tightly.' On an exchange to the University of Missouri it was taken for granted that as a novelist Francis could – and would – teach creative writing as well as American literature. To his surprise, he found it very rewarding.

Well, he reflects, you may not be able to teach people to write but you can take people who are capable of writing and provide them with the space and structure within which they have to write. In contrast to the growing number of creative writing programmes around the country, students at Manchester are required to complete an entire novel, rather than a series of short stories. It has been a constant source of friction with the university authorities – 60,000 words is a very long thesis, after all.

Less controversial but no less vital is the academic content – something often missing from courses elsewhere, notes Schmidt, diplomatically declining to point the finger. The course has four components, the central and most crucial of which are workshops.

Four times a year, students produce 5,000 words of their novel for discussion and criticism. Although intimidating, the sessions were invaluable for Anna Davis, who was among the first intake of students and has since secured a two-book deal with Sceptre. Her superb first novel, *The Dinner*, is to be published in January.

She says: 'Writers are terribly alone in their work – it's very difficult to get people to read you and give you decent feedback. On a course, you've got a captive audience to give you proper attention.' Learning to put her work on the line and accept criticism prepared her well for the onerous world of agents and editors. Between workshops, students study twelve divergent course texts. They also complete a practical project, such as translating a novel or adapting one for the screen. Finally, there is a vocational component, when students learn about the publishing industry from the inside, studying contracts, copyright law, profit and loss accounting, writing blurbs and advance information sheets for their novels.

Schmidt is a publisher himself – owner of Carcanet Press and editor of the poetry magazine PN Review. He says: 'Most novelists tie up their manuscript with a pretty ribbon in the assumption the industry eagerly awaits their work, whereas, of course, the last thing publishers and agents look forward to is a huge slush-pile slithering through their door. If nothing else, the course gives them a degree of scepticism and realistic expectation.'

Not only does the vocational element teach students how to package their ideas and sell themselves, it also prepares many for a career within the industry itself. After graduation, Anna Davis got a job assisting the managing-director at one of the larger literary agencies, David Higham.

Today, when she's not finishing off her second novel, she works part-time for another large literary agent, Curtis Brown. In the ceaseless bid to discover new talent, many former students working in the industry have kept in touch with their old tutors. Touring the universities giving guest lectures, they can meet and greet students and attempt to sniff out tomorrow's prizewinners. Last year, Lee Braxton, assistant to Faber's fiction editor, was in Manchester to talk to MA students. Francis suggested he drop in on another class, where by chance he met Clare Wigfall. After reading two of her short stories, he snapped up the twenty-one year old. He has his eye on another three or four writers, but refuses to elaborate.

'When we started this MA,' said Francis, 'I thought publishers would look down on us as amateurs, but that couldn't be further from the truth. Courses like Manchester's are adding an important new dimension to British publishing.'

For questions **17–22**, you must choose which of the paragraphs **A–G** on page **81** fit into the numbered gaps in the following magazine article. There is one extra paragraph which does not fit in any of the gaps.

Indicate your answers **on the separate answer sheet**.

Terrorised by a Collar Stud The Worst of Times

Glen Baxter talks to Danny Danziger

I had a terrible stammer from about nine to 18, when I went to a speech therapist who cured me. So there are a few hellish years in there. Because there are certain words you stumble over, you do anything rather than hit against those words right away, so you would invent ways of asking for things, you found little phrases which helped.

17

The stammer was pretty bad. I was unable to go on buses and pay the correct fare, because the correct fare was sixpence, which I couldn't say – at least not before I got to my destination. And as I could say eightpence, that was easier. I'd pay eightpence.

18

Anyway, I went into this shop and I was standing at the counter for ages and ages, and I finally

said. 'U-d-do you have any c-c-collar st-st-studs? And the man in the furniture shop, which was next door to the haberdashery shop – I'd gone into the wrong shop – he said. 'I am really sorry, but we haven't got any left, but if you pop next door they might have one or two.'

19

But of course the more you think about it the worse it gets, so by the time I actually arrived at the shop, I was a complete jibbering wreck.

When I was in junior school there was this pressure to pass the 11-plus examination. My brother had passed it.

20

I didn't have any staying power. I couldn't concentrate on anything if things were boring. I was under pressure to get the 11-plus and get out of there, and I guess it must have been a bit too much. I was very good at English but when they collected the English exam, I had turned over two pages by mistake, so there were two pages I hadn't done. The headmaster just said, more or less, 'That's it', and I was devastated.

21

So I passed the exam, but I still had the stammer, and I then went to see a speech therapist.

22

If I meet somebody who stammers, I start to do it unconsciously, and if I talk about stammering – it's building up in me now – I'll start stammering in a minute.

A My brother was very clever, people always wanted me to be more like my brother and do well at school, but I was a nuisance, chattering and mucking about and not being serious about subjects, and I just used to love drawing all the time.

B She got us all to lie down on the floor and let our toes relax, and then consecutively everything else, and my mother used to do it with me in the evenings: half an hour of lying on the floor just relaxing – and it seemed to work.

C Like going into a shop for oranges: if I wanted to buy an orange, I'd say, 'Uh, by the way, do you happen to have any oranges?' I couldn't just say, 'Can I have an orange please?' And of course if you go into a shop which is full of oranges and say 'Uh, by the way, do you have any oranges?', of course they've got oranges, I mean, it's completely ridiculous, and so I spent a lot of my childhood in this crazy atmosphere.

D But I was the only boy to get the 11-plus out of that entire school. And when I went to grammar school, there were lads in my class and girls too, from schools where 95% of everyone who took the 11-plus automatically passed.

E You either passed the 11-plus and got out of that school or you became one of these big lumps who used to hang around. And if you were fat, or if you had got a stammer, you were bound to be bullied. Kids are cruel, aren't they?

F I remember once my parents told me to go to the haberdashery shop to get a collar stud for my dad's shirt. It was probably just a mission to get me out of the house, looking back on it now.

G He was very, very nice about it. In my panic about having to say 'collar stud' on my way there, I'd been thinking: now when I go into the shop I've got to be careful not to say collar stud straightaway.

Read the following newspaper article and then answer questions **23–28** on page **83**. On your answer sheet, indicate the letter **A**, **B**, **C** or **D** against the number of each question, **23–28**. Give only one answer to each question.

Indicate your answers **on the separate answer sheet**.

Desert Discoveries and Monster Myths

DAVID KEYS on new insights into the day of the dinosaur.

Chinese and Canadian scientists working in the Gobi Desert have stumbled across a series of 80-million-year-old dinosaur colonies – including one with a dozen 150-centimetre-long babies, and another with five tiny embryos. These perfectly preserved, uncrushed skeletons are now helping experts study the range of facial and other physical differences displayed by dinosaurs within a single species. Because all the babies are of the same colony, they are certain to be of the same species and must therefore have a common gene pool. Detailed examination is revealing marked differences between individual colony members, with some of them having broader or larger faces than others.

The new data emerging from this and related research have serious implications for dinosaur studies in general. In the past, differences in head size and shape have often led palaeontologists to conclude that they had discovered new species. But now that it is known that great physical variations can occur within a single dinosaur colony, experts fear that many of the 500 listed dinosaur species on the fossil record may not be separate species after all.

The Gobi Desert colony discovered this year is of a species of vegetarian armoured dinosaur known as an ankylosaur. Finds so far include a large number of eggs, the babies, some adults and a group of embryos – each only 36 centimetres long. Excavations have provided snapshots of daily life in an ankylosaur colony, including what appears to have been an attack by a carnivorous dinosaur on the ankylosaur nest full of eggs. The fossilised predator is preserved lying on top of the egg-filled nest, and seems to have perished as a result of a sand storm which buried both the hunter and its prey.

The Sino-Canadian team excavating several Gobi sites has unearthed eggs belonging to numerous dinosaur species. Some appear to have produced the strangest of eggs in the strangest of ways. Ankylosaur eggs, for example were neither round nor oval, but long and thin – around 180 centimetres long and 60 centimetres in diameter. Ankylosaur females seem to have laid them with great efficiency, two at a time. One extraordinary nest, containing thirty of these eggs, has yielded some clues about laying techniques. The eggs were arranged in the nest in a multi-layer spiral, resembling a pyramid. It seems that the female dug the nest with her hind legs, then laid pairs of eggs as she proceeded around it.

The team has also unearthed the skull and vertebrae of what seems to be the Old World's largest dinosaur. From the remains unearthed, palaeontologists have been able to calculate that the creature was 31 metres from head to tail – ten per cent longer than any other Old World dinosaur found so far. Related to a dinosaur called mamenchisaurus – but as yet unnamed in its own right – it lived around 140 million years ago, was vegetarian, weighed up to forty tonnes and would probably have walked at less than sixteen kilometres per hour.

China's dinosaur discoveries cover the entire epoch of dinosaur prevalence on Earth – from around 225 million to 65 million years ago. In the end they were wiped out by a natural disaster, possibly caused by meteorite impact. Detailed study from fossil material found in China, and in North America, is helping to prove that many of the later dinosaurs had comparatively large brains, mammal-style binocular vision and more complex behaviour than previously thought. They were not, it seems, always the dumb giants they are normally portrayed as being.

23   The dinosaur finds mentioned in paragraph one are yielding new information because

   A   they contain baby dinosaurs.
   B   the skeletons are undamaged.
   C   they are 80 million years old.
   D   the dinosaurs are exceptionally large.

24   According to paragraph two, what are the implications for dinosaur research?

   A   For the first time head size and shape can be studied.
   B   A new species has been identified.
   C   The estimated number of dinosaur species will be modified.
   D   The idea of how dinosaurs looked is being changed.

25   Which of the following is true of the ankylosaur?

   A   It ate eggs as a basic part of its diet.
   B   It produced eggs of an unusual shape.
   C   Males and females incubated the eggs.
   D   It defended its eggs against attack.

26   What did the ankylosaur do when producing its young?

   A   It improved on a nest already made by other dinosaur species.
   B   It used its back legs to produce a hole in the ground.
   C   It positioned its eggs carefully with the use of its front legs.
   D   It laid each egg on top of another.

27   The scientists have discovered a large dinosaur which is

   A   about to be given a new name.
   B   the biggest ever found outside America.
   C   complete except for the head and tail.
   D   related to another Chinese dinosaur.

28   What do the recent Chinese discoveries of dinosaurs show?

   A   They lived for longer than had previously been thought.
   B   Their eyesight was different from what had been believed.
   C   Their large brains allowed them to move quickly.
   D   They declined gradually over a period of several centuries.

Answer questions **29–46** by referring to the newspaper article about holidays on pages **85–86**.

Indicate your answers **on the separate answer sheet**.

For questions **29–46** choose your answers from the list of people (**A–F**) on the right below.

Some choices may be required more than once.

Note: When more than one answer is required, these may be given **in any order**.

Who

dislikes the idea of relaxing?	**29**				
helped a friend in difficulty?	**30**				
appreciated the simple life?	**31**				
received understanding from family members?	**32**				
were forced to repeat the same experience in following years?	**33**	**34**		**A**	Bill Bryson
failed to take the necessary precautions?	**35**			**B**	Naim Attallah
pretended to be enjoying things?	**36**			**C**	Ines de la Fresange
enjoyed getting some exercise?	**37**			**D**	Quentin Crisp
was in a place with facilities that were not appreciated?	**38**			**E**	Maureen Lipman
found activities were dependent on the weather?	**39**			**F**	Malcolm McLaren
went on holiday at a time that was not the best?	**40**				
was obliged to do something dangerous?	**41**				
were forced into the holiday?	**42**	**43**	**44**		
had a parent whose feelings about the place were similar?	**45**				
was a victim of unfriendly animals?	**46**				

Best of Times, Worst of Times

turning into a nightmare and we went home immediately. My wife and son were not upset because they know my nature.

Ines de la Fresange
Model

When I was seven I was sent to boarding school in England to learn English during the summer holidays. The school was supposed to be a paradise for children. There was a tennis court, a swimming pool and horses, but I hated tennis, thought it was too cold to swim and was afraid of horses. The school was filled with foreigners learning English, but I was very shy and didn't like the other children. I cried all the time and wrote long letters to my grandmother saying I was lonely. As I was quite tiny, my family decided that my nanny should stay in a nearby hotel for the month I was at school. I was allowed to see her on Sundays when she took me to her hotel which was full of old people who danced at teatime. I remember crying and crying on Sunday evenings when I had to catch the bus back. It was a nightmare for a child, but I was sent back several years running because my family was obsessed with my learning English.

Bill Bryson
Travel writer

The happiest holiday I ever had was on Lundy Island with my wife and three children. It is run by the Landmark Trust, and unspoilt. There are no towns or shops and nothing to do but go for invigorating walks and look for puffins. The island generates its own electricity which is turned off at 10 o'clock at night. Having tucked the children up in bed, we would build a roaring fire in our little cottage and read by the firelight. It was perfect.

Quentin Crisp
Writer

All my childhood holidays were nightmares. My family had a cottage near Hastings on the south coast where we went year after year, and it was absolute hell. I went for the whole summer with my mother and brothers and sisters. My father came down for two weeks: he hated everything. It was no holiday for my mother. She had to cut sandwiches for us all and carry them to the beach. There were wasps everywhere and sand in everything. I can't understand why we didn't eat at home and then go and sit on the beach. I pretended I loved the seaside because I wanted to be like

Naim Attallah
Publisher

I hardly ever take holidays but fourteen years ago I was pressurised into going to the Costa Smeralda with my wife and son. I enjoyed the first day: I hired a boat, sat in the sun for about twenty minutes and had tea on the veranda. By the second the novelty of doing nothing had worn off. I love the bustle of towns and my excitement comes from working. I can't stand people who appear lazy. All I could see were people sitting and frying in the sun. I got very agitated: the holiday was other people, but I never succeeded. I got on with my brothers and sisters in a half-hearted way, but they teased me unmercifully. We went on jolly outings when it wasn't raining. I'm no good at sport and I can't ride a bike. When I was eleven the cottage was sold and we stopped going, which was a great relief to me.

Maureen Lipman
Actress

This year my husband Jack and I went skiing in Switzerland with the actress Julia McKenzie and her husband Gerry. Although the holiday was a laugh, the skiing part was a nightmare. It probably wasn't the best time to learn: we clock up about two hundred years between us. It was also April and there wasn't much snow, just lots of hardpacked ice. Jack, who has got his hip and his head screwed on, refused to go near the slopes; Gerry could ski a bit and went into the big boys' class, Julia and I started on the nursery slopes. I could snow plough, but Julia kept skiing into a fence. I had to pick her up, which is not easy when you're over forty and have big wooden things on your feet. After she had fallen several times, Julia gave up and headed for the restaurant. I was more foolhardy, and went up the mountain with the rest of the class. Our instructor told us to ski down. After a couple of zig-zags my heart was pounding. I took off my skis and said, "I'm walking." It took me an hour and a half to get down. I reached a farm and was attacked by three dogs. By the time someone came to call them off, I was terrified and weeping. When I reached the bottom I could hardly speak.

Malcolm McLaren
Record Producer

While I was an art student I decided to travel to Libya and halfway there I realised I'd forgotten to have the jabs. I was courting Vivienne Westwood at the time and she joined me in Marseilles. We slept in a tent on the beach, and one morning we woke up to discover we were floating in the middle of the ocean. We found a sympathetic baker who let us dry out by his ovens, but we lost everything – it had all floated away. We had no money, and I thieved fruit and sardines from the local market so we could eat. There was a bullring in Marseilles and if you stayed in the ring with the bull for a certain length of time you got fifty francs. I did it because we were desperate, but I was terrified.

PAPER 2   Writing (2 hours)

1   You have organised a one-day tennis tournament between the language school where you are studying and another school. You have received a letter and telephone message which have caused you to make changes at short notice. You have contacted people by phone and have made new arrangements.

Read the original timetable for the one-day tournament, the telephone message and the letter. Then, **using the information carefully**, write **an information leaflet** that will attract members of the public to the tournament and which gives full information about the new arrangements.

Write approximately 250 words. You should use your own words as far as possible.

SPECIAL ONE DAY TENNIS TOURNAMENT

Melchester School of English
v
Exonbury International Students' Club

Saturday 7th July

10.30 Arrival. Coffee.

11.00 Play commences. Under 16 matches.

1.00 Lunch.

2.00 Open matches (all ages).

6.00 Presentation of prizes by Sir Philip Delaunay
(Wimbledon champion 1950–52).

7.00 Dinner followed by dancing.

10.00 End of tournament.

Letter

… and of course I shall be delighted to present the prizes for your club. I always look forward to meeting young tennis players and encouraging them in this wonderful sport. I regret that, owing to prior engagement, I will not be able to arrive until shortly before 6 p.m. but I hope to stay until the end of the tournament.

Yours sincerely,

Sir Philip Delaunay

Telephone message

Secretary of Exonbury International Students' Club phoned. Some problems! Team can't arrive until 12 noon and must leave by 6.30 p.m. – problems with roadworks on motorway, journey will take longer than usual. Also, no under 16 players this time. Can you rearrange things? Please contact.

Choose **one** of the following writing tasks. Your answer should follow exactly the instructions given. Write approximately 250 words.

2   You have been asked to write an article for a series in an English Language newspaper. A number of people have been asked to write the same kind of article. You have to describe some or all of the following: the happiest moment of your life, your greatest fear, your greatest regret, your favourite journey and which single thing would most improve the quality of your life. Write a lively and interesting article that readers of the newspaper will enjoy reading.

Write your **article**.

3   A friend of yours who you met while studying in Britain has now returned to his / her own country. He / she has written to you expressing fears about the future. He / she is mainly concerned about war, pollution, and unemployment. Write a letter to your friend which will reassure him / her. You should take an optimistic view of the future.

Write your **letter**.

4   You have entered a competition and the prize is either a first-class round-the-world air ticket, valid for one year plus all accommodation expenses paid for you, or a one-year stay in another country of your choice, with all accommodation expenses paid for you plus a free language course in the language of that country. As part of the competition you have to write a letter to the competition organisers saying which prize you would prefer, and why.

Write your **letter**.

5   You have been asked by the manager of a company in Britain for which you work, to stay in a hotel for two days and then write a report on the hotel, mentioning positive and negative aspects. Comment on the location, the room, the facilities available and the service. Say whether the hotel is a suitable place for business people to stay.

Write your **report**.

PAPER 3 English in Use (1 hour 30 minutes)

For questions **1–15**, read the text below and then decide which word best fits each space. Put the letter you choose for each question in the correct box on your answer sheet. The exercise begins with an example (**0**).

Example: 0 ℬ | 0

You Must Remember This ...

Sometimes you might feel that if you had a perfect memory, all your problems with learning would be (**0**) .... . You would be able to (**1**) .... through exams without much revision. You would never again (**2**) .... the embarrassment of forgetting someone's name. But imagine, for a moment, not forgetting anything – not even last year's shopping (**3**) .... You would be (**4**) .... with information.

With hard work you can recall the parts of a verb or the layout of a town as you need them, so that you can learn a foreign language or (**5**) .... a taxi driver's licence. But the memory (**6**) .... called for by some professions are only one of the roles memory plays in our lives. Memory covers a (**7**) .... range of actions and needs. What we (**8**) .... about the brain is far from complete, so philosophers and scientists find it difficult to be (**9**) .... about the nature of memory. Remembering and forgetting can be understood in many different (**10**) .... but broadly, three distinct classes of memory have been established: personal, cognitive and habit memory.

Personal memories are those acts of remembering which (**11**) .... specifically to each person's life history. If you say, 'I remember the first time I travelled by train', you will probably have an image in your mind of the (**12**) .... and be able to describe things in it. Cognitive memory helps us learn, for example, stories, a speech or a (**13**) .... of music. Habit memory (**14**) .... those abilities needed to perform actions such as typing or driving. All these actions must be learned but once they have been, you will rarely remember anything (**15**) .... as you perform them.

0	**A**	answered	**B**	solved	**C**	improved	**D**	removed
1	**A**	sail	**B**	walk	**C**	run	**D**	float
2	**A**	encounter	**B**	face	**C**	realise	**D**	accept
3	**A**	receipts	**B**	notes	**C**	lists	**D**	bills
4	**A**	overweight	**B**	stuffed	**C**	burdened	**D**	overloaded
5	**A**	win	**B**	gain	**C**	earn	**D**	award
6	**A**	concepts	**B**	choices	**C**	feats	**D**	methods
7	**A**	wide	**B**	large	**C**	long	**D**	big
8	**A**	study	**B**	learn	**C**	discover	**D**	know
9	**A**	precise	**B**	explanatory	**C**	correct	**D**	aware
10	**A**	ways	**B**	concepts	**C**	forms	**D**	types
11	**A**	connect	**B**	appear	**C**	have	**D**	refer
12	**A**	occasion	**B**	happening	**C**	process	**D**	thought
13	**A**	piece	**B**	tune	**C**	sound	**D**	instrument
14	**A**	means	**B**	covers	**C**	enables	**D**	directs
15	**A**	totally	**B**	hardly	**C**	knowingly	**D**	consciously

For questions **16–30** complete the following article by writing each missing word in the correct box on your answer sheet. **Use only one word for each space.** The exercise begins with an example (**0**).

Example:

0	*was*		0
			☐ ▨

The Development of the Motor Car

The earliest motor vehicle (**0**) .... built in 1769 by Nicolas-Joseph Cugnot. It was powered by steam and (**16**) .... a top speed of about four kph. Many similar vehicles were then built, mainly (**17**) .... use on farms. These steam wagons had a sturdy frame and heavy wooden wheels. This made them capable (**18**) .... carrying heavy loads. By 1865 in response to growing public fears that steam vehicles were travelling too fast, (**19**) .... speed limit was introduced. (**20**) .... was decided that three kph in towns and six kph in country areas was fast (**21**) .... As an additional safety precaution, a person waving a red flag had to walk in front of the vehicle. You (**22**) .... think that (**23**) .... speed limit was very low, but you must remember that the roads were very poor and that many steam vehicles found (**24**) .... difficult to stop quickly.

In 1885, Carl Benz built the Motorwagon, the first car to have a petrol engine. It was (**25**) .... lighter than the steam engine and (**26**) .... travel at fifteen kph. (**27**) .... type of vehicle was considered less dangerous than the large, heavy steam wagons. In 1896, the speed limit for petrol-driven cars was raised to 22 kph and in 1903 it reached 32 kph.

In Detroit in 1903 the Ford Motor Company was founded. By 1908 Ford was mass-producing (**28**) .... famous Model T cars on an assembly line. This meant that the time and cost of car-making was dramatically reduced and more people could afford to buy (**29**) .... own car. There are now 23 million cars in the United Kingdom and the average person makes thirteen journeys a week, most of (**30**) .... by road.

In **most** lines of the following text, there is either a spelling or a punctuation error. For each numbered line **31–46** write the correctly spelled word or show the correct punctuation. Some lines are correct. Indicate these lines with a tick (✓). The exercise begins with three examples (**0**).

Examples:

0	*doubt*	0
00	*emotions that*	0
000	✓	0

Why do people sometimes fail to help when they should?

0	....	There is little dout that people exist who simply do not feel
00	....	the emotions, that are felt by ordinary people. Because of a
000	....	brain defect or some other kind of abnormality, they lack
31	....	empathy. They cannot feel another human beings pain,
32	....	either emotional or physical. Fortunatly, they are a rarity.
33	....	More common are decent, normal, people who, at one time
34	....	or another fail to help somebody who, in retrospect, obviously
35	....	needed help. In one infamous case in New York in 1964,
36	....	thirty eight people had a chance to interrupt a murder in
37	....	progress but did not. Why such things happen has perplexed
38	....	philosophers for centaries and today psychologists have joined
39	....	the search for answers? One general rule is that the better we
40	....	know someone or the more he or she is like us, the more likely
41	....	we are to help that person. We seldome hesitate to help people
42	....	we love. However we often think twice about helping strangers,
43	....	especially if they are diferent from ourselves. Oddly, a victim's
44	....	chances of being promptly helped seem to decrease as the number
45	....	of people observing the Emergency increases. Bystanders tend
46	....	to think that somebody else has already made a decision about
		what to do and that further help is on its way or unnecessary.

For questions **47–61** read the two texts below. Use the words in the boxes to the right of the texts to form **one** word that fits in the same numbered space in the text. Write the new word in the correct box on your answer sheet. The exercise begins with an example (**0**).

Example:	0	*safely*		0

A NEWSPAPER REPORT

Terrified Customers

A TWO-METRE-LONG green and yellow snake is (**0**) .... in police custody after terrified customers fled in panic when they saw it crawling along the fresh-fruit counter of a local supermarket. Police officers who were called to the scene found a very (**47**) .... and agitated snake and managed to capture it with some (**48**) .... Police Constable John Brown said, "It was very (**49**) .... and quite heavy and it took three of us to put it in a large bag. We think it may belong to a snake (**50**) .... and could have escaped from a parked car. We'd like the owner to contact us and help us with our (**51**) ...." The snake was examined by a vet who said that it was well-fed, perfectly healthy but rather (**52**) .... He confirmed that it was not (**53**) ....

(0)	SAFE
(47)	NERVE
(48)	DIFFICULT
(49)	SLIP
(50)	ENTHUSE
(51)	ENQUIRE
(52)	FRIEND
(53)	POISON

AN INFORMATION LEAFLET

Personal Presentation

When you have accepted our offer of (**54**) .... you will be issued, free of charge, with a uniform which you are obliged to wear while on duty. Our uniform has been designed after detailed (**55**) .... with members of staff and reflects the quality and style of our business. It helps to form the customers' first (**56**) .... of us. Please note that male staff are not permitted to wear (**57**) .... of any kind and female staff must not wear rings or earrings which are (**58**) .... large or could be regarded as (**59**) .... in shape or design. Wristwatches are permitted but must be (**60**) .... in size and appearance. If in doubt, talk to your line manager. For both men and women, hair should not exceed shoulder (**61**) ....

(54)	EMPLOY
(55)	CONSULT
(56)	IMPRESS
(57)	JEWEL
(58)	EXCESS
(59)	APPROPRIATE
(60)	ACCEPT
(61)	LONG

For questions **62–74**, read the following newspaper story and use the information in it to complete the numbered gaps in the informal letter. Then write the new words in the correct space on your answer sheet. **Use no more than two words for each gap.** The words you need **do not occur** in the newspaper story. The exercise begins with an example (**0**).

Example:

0	*country*	0
		☐ ▨

Superdog Shot in Mouth – But Survives!
Thugs licked by plucky Alsatian

The rustic peace of the quaint old village of Petersham, in leafy Surrey, where the posh folks live, was shattered yesterday. Two armed raiders, brandishing a shotgun and revolver, burst into the post-office, run by Mr Walter Wall, 52, and demanded he give them cash. Customers quaked with fear, but plucky guard dog Zorro dashed out from under the counter, bared his fangs and sank them into the leg of one of the raiders, who screamed with pain. His cowardly companion then blasted hero-dog Zorro at point-blank range – BUT THE BULLETS BOUNCED OFF ZORRO'S ROCK-HARD GNASHERS! Nonplussed, the raiders fled empty-handed. Police caught them after a high-speed car chase. A pall of fear now hangs heavy over the strife-torn village that was once Petersham.

Wonder-dog Zorro was whisked off for emergency treatment. A top vet said, 'He's going to be all right.'

INFORMAL LETTER

Dear Jack,

You'll never believe what has happened here. I'm enclosing a press cutting for you. It's the sort of thing you expect to happen in the inner city rather than here in the (**0**) .... Maybe they thought that because the people who live here are quite (**62**) .... , there would be plenty of money to steal.

I was in the Post Office when two men rushed in. (**63**) .... them had a gun, which he (**64**) .... Mr Wall, (**65**) .... , began to (**66**) .... the money, as they had told him. Some of the customers were so frightened they were (**67**) .... At that moment Mr Wall's dog, Zorro, who had been quietly lying on the (**68**) .... , jumped up and (**69**) .... one of the robbers, causing him to scream in agony. The other robber shot Zorro at close range. Amazingly, the bullets bounced off Zorro's (**70**) .... ! The robbers were extremely (**71**) .... by this and ran out without (**72**) .... Zorro was (**73**) .... taken to a vet for treatment. Apparently, he (**74**) .... soon, which is good news, isn't it?

Best wishes,

Paul

For questions **75–80**, read through the following text and then choose from the list **A–J** below the best phrase to fill each of the spaces. Write one letter (**A–J**) in the correct box on your answer sheet. **Some of the suggested answers do not fit at all.** The exercise begins with an example (**0**).

Example: | 0 | *J* | 0 ▭ ▬ |

Aspects of Love

For Dr Robert Sternberg, a psychologist at Yale University, love has no mystery. He has dedicated almost a decade of research to dissecting love, examining in a scientific way why people fall in and out of love. He has reached conclusions (**0**) .... . In fact, he has formulated Sternberg's Triangular Theory of Love (**75**) .... . The first is intimacy (**76**) .... . The second is passion, which includes excitement and arousal. Thirdly, there is decision and commitment, (**77**) .... : the decision to love someone and the pledge to nurse that love through good and bad times. The way you combine these three components dictates the type of love you experience. Intimacy alone results in an unspectacular liking, while passion alone generates an infatuated crush. Overdo the decision and commitment and you end up with what Dr Sternberg calls 'empty love' (**78**) .... . Complete the triangle by pledging everlasting devotion and you enjoy consummate love (**79**) .... . Fortunately, differences in the three different styles of love are treatable. Sternberg says the answer is quite simple. If your partner craves more intimacy, passion or commitment, then you must identify (**80**) .... and do your best to provide more of it – if you want to keep your partner, that is.

A   which is typical of the stages of an affair
B   which component is missing
C   which is the best of all according to Dr Sternberg's theory
D   which is a common symptom of an exhausted or dying love affair
E   which he defines as a sharing of thoughts and feelings
F   which has three components
G   which is made up of two parts
H   which Sternberg is hoping to
I   which is what your partner wants

J   which enable him to predict the long-term success of romantic entanglements

PART 1

You will hear someone describing a traffic accident that he saw. For questions **1–10**, complete the notes below, using one or two words.

You will hear the recording twice.

An Accident At The Roundabout

Position of witness: [_____ | **1**] hotel room on 20th floor

Vehicles involved in accident:

type [_____ | **2**]   colour [_____ | **3**]

type [_____ | **4**]   colour [_____ | **5**]

On the roundabout one car was hit [_____ | **6**] on the side.

Other vehicles mentioned: [_____ | **7**] lorry

[_____ | **8**] car

Number of vehicles that stopped after the accident: [_____ | **9**]

Witness thought one driver might have been [_____ | **10**]

PART 2

You will hear an astronomer talking about the planet Mars. For questions **11–20**, complete the table with the missing information. For each answer you will have to write down a number or a word.

Listen very carefully as you will hear the recording ONCE only.

The Red Planet

MARS: The Facts

Diameter of Mars: | **11** | kilometres

Percentage of Earth's gravity: | **12**

Percentage of Earth's sunlight: | **13**

Length of Martian year: | **14** | Earth days

Length of Martian day: | hours | minutes | **15**

Number of moons: | **16**

Compared with Earth's moon, they are:

| **17**

Atmosphere consists mainly of | **18**

Percentage of oxygen: | **19**

Highest volcano: | **20** | metres

PART 3

You will hear a radio programme in which two people, Marcia and Robert, talk about the differences between electronic book discs and conventional printed books. During the interview they express various views. For questions **21–30**, indicate which views are expressed by Marcia and which are expressed by Robert, by writing **M** (for Marcia) or **R** (for Robert) in the box provided. You may write both initials in one box if both express the same view.

You will hear the recording twice.

Electronic Books

CD-ROM discs are more convenient to use than printed books. | 21

Disc books are lighter than paperback books. | 22

It is quicker to obtain information from printed books than from computers. | 23

Handheld computers use up batteries very quickly. | 24

Only reference books are suitable in electronic format. | 25

The quality of the image on computer screens is poor. | 26

Electronic book discs take up less space than printed books. | 27

There is no worldwide standard for electronic book discs. | 28

Printed books are cheaper than electronic book discs. | 29

Bookshops will not exist in the future. | 30

You will hear **five** short extracts in which different people talk about danger and risk in their lives.

Danger And Risk

TASK ONE

For questions **31–35**, match the extracts as you hear them with the people, listed **A–H**.

A   police officer

B   firefighter

	31

C   mountain rescuer

	32

D   film stuntman

	33

E   helicopter pilot

	34

F   racing driver

G   parachutist

	35

H   caver

TASK TWO

For questions **36–40**, match the extracts as you hear them with the reasons given by each speaker for taking part in dangerous activities, listed **A–H**.

A   working in a team

B   sense of duty

	36

C   variety

	37

D   excitement

	38

E   saving lives

	39

F   self-control

G   technical skill

	40

H   money

Remember that you must complete both tasks as you listen. You will hear the recording twice.

PAPER 5

Speaking (15 minutes)

PART 1 (3 minutes)

Answer these questions:

What kind of holidays do you like to have?
What was your best holiday ever?
Is there a kind of holiday that you would like to try but haven't yet?
Do you prefer to relax on holiday or to take part in a lot of activities?

PART 2 (3 or 4 minutes)

Audiences (Describe, identify and speculate)

Turn to pictures 1–5 on page 138 which show different audiences.

Candidate A, describe people in three of the pictures and say how they are reacting to the show. You have a minute to do this.

Candidate B, can you tell us which three pictures candidate A described?

Ruins (Describe, eliminate and speculate)

Turn to pictures 1–5 on page 139 which show ruined places.

Candidate B, describe three of these places, saying why people like to visit them. You have a minute to do this.

Candidate A, can you tell us which two ruins candidate B did not describe?

PART 3 (3 or 4 minutes)

Souvenirs (Discuss, evaluate and select)

Turn to pictures 1–7 on page 140 which show things which are sold to tourists in London as souvenirs.

What image of London do they convey? Which do you think is the best and the worst?

PART 4 (3 or 4 minutes)

Answer these questions:

Did you reach agreement?
How do your opinions differ?
Which souvenir would you choose and why?
What kind of things are good or bad souvenirs of your own town or country?

TEST 5

Reading (1 hour 15 minutes)

PART 1

Answer questions **1–17** by referring to the newspaper article about argument and debate on page **101**.

Indicate your answers **on the separate answer sheet**.

For questions **1–17**, answer by choosing from the sections of the article (**A–G**).

You may choose any of the sections more than once.

Note: When more than one answer is required, these may be given **in any order**.

Which section refers to the following?

ways in which public opinion was formed in the past	**1** ....
a book from which we can learn the skills of arguing	**2** ....
a reference to old ideas about education	**3** ....
a suggestion that ancient orators were superior to modern ones	**4** ....
the best starting point for developing arguments	**5** ....
a very good way to influence an audience with your arguments	**6** ....
suggests two different methods for presenting the points of an argument	**7** ....
mentions important factors apart from the arguments themselves	**8** .... **9** ....
emphasises the importance of thinking for yourself	**10** ....
someone who was familiar with ideas from ancient times	**11** ....
a popular misconception that the writer disagrees with	**12** ....
positive and peaceful aspects of arguing	**13** ....
the idea that good arguments are always organised according to the same pattern	**14** ....
a criticism of speaking without preparation	**15** ....
the reason why speaking well was a valuable skill in the ancient world	**16** ....
a slightly sceptical view of one group of public speakers	**17** ....

The Power Of The Spoken Word

Arguments and debates can be exhilarating experiences. But those wishing to be more persuasive must first make sure they prepare.

A

If you say "I am having an argument", most people will assume that you are picking a fight. But this need not necessarily be so. The ability to argue in a controlled way is a fundamental skill. It is used by lawyers, politicians, campaigners and many others every day of the week. Arguing well is part of the process of successful negotiation. It is far more likely to get you out of trouble than into it. Some people instinctively find that they are strong arguers. However, the art of arguing can be taught, and in many schools it is part of other subjects. Until the beginning of this century, many people considered arguing to be one of the essential elements in a proper education.

B

The Greeks and Romans, whose ideas about law, science, the arts and society have had such an enormous impact on our own culture, also influenced the way we argue. Aristotle (384–322 BC), the Greek philosopher, wrote a work called *Rhetorica* which laid down rules to follow in order to argue successfully. In these ancient societies, writing was used less widely than in ours and so public speaking was very important. There were no newspapers and no television to help people decide what they thought about issues. Practised speakers, known as orators, who spoke on formal occasions and at public meetings, were critical in helping to form opinions. Orators used all the tricks of rhetoric to get their points across. In Shakespeare's play *Julius Caesar*, Mark Antony is so angry about the assassination of Caesar, his friend, that he makes a powerful speech to the Roman people. Shakespeare, who knew from his reading about the Roman art of public speaking, gives his character powerful lines which win the people over to his side. Speaking like a true Roman orator, Antony addresses his audience with the lines, "Friends, Romans, countrymen, lend me your ears …"

C

If Anthony were transported in time and space to the Houses of Parliament in Britain today, he would almost certainly recognise what was going on. He would realise that when politicians "debate" bills or motions, they are following on from the lines that were laid down in the ancient world. Whether he would be impressed by what he heard is, of course, another matter.

D

To win an argument, you need to convince someone that you are right. To do that you have to make a good case, which requires organisation. Many people have suggested ways to do this. The same basic principles underlie most systems. Firstly, you should decide what you think. It is surprising how many people start sounding off about something without really deciding what they think about it. An opinion which has been formed without any real thought or inherited from others – friends or parents, for example – is really no more than a prejudice. Before you are able to argue on any subject, you need to understand what you are talking about.

E

Next, you should select your arguments. The whole process of talking about your opinion and showing why it is right is known as an argument. The individual parts of the process are also called arguments. Selecting your arguments means coming up with the reasons which best support your opinion. It often helps to think of specific examples to help illustrate them. You might want to argue that nuclear power should be banned. One of your arguments might be that it is dangerous. You might want to illustrate this by giving examples of accidents that have actually happened.

F

You should also anticipate your opponent's arguments because, as well as coming up with reasons in support of your opinion, you need to think about the criticisms that might be made of it. You need answers for these criticisms. This is one of the most powerful ways of winning over your audience.

G

The order of your arguments is also very important. You might want to deal with the powerful and convincing arguments first. On the other hand, you might like to start with the less important ones and build up a more and more convincing case. Of course, there is more to winning an argument than just having a good case. You also need to present it properly. That means not just thinking about what you say, but also about how you say it. Over the years, people have thought up a number of techniques to make what they say persuasive. These include asking rhetorical questions (which are not meant to be answered), appealing to the audience's emotions and making effective analogies.

For questions **18–23**, you must choose which of the paragraphs **A–G** on page **103** fit into the numbered gaps in the following magazine article. There is one extra paragraph which does not fit in any of the gaps.

Indicate your answers **on the separate answer sheet**.

Simply the best

"You've got to go for it, you can't just expect things to drop into your lap." Marie Orpen's philosophy could help to explain how she has become the UK Top Secretary at the tender age of 23, beating 500 other candidates nationwide. The title of Top Secretary is awarded annually by the London Chamber of Commerce and Industry's Examinations Board (LCCIEB) to the candidate who both achieves the highest marks in its Private and Executive Secretary's Diploma (PESD) and can convince a panel of judges that they are senior PA material. Orpen's five distinctions in the PESD last year guaranteed her a place on the shortlist of five high achievers invited to London in November for the interview, where the secretaries had to demonstrate their skills across areas including commercial awareness and diplomacy.

| 18 |

Orpen works as a personal secretary to a senior manager in the IT services division of the Post Office. It is her first job and she got it straight after leaving Farnborough College of Technology with the PESD last summer. She is convinced she would not have been taken on to such a high-level position without those letters on her CV. Her boss, Karen Foster, recognised the Diploma and realised she'd be capable of more than just typing, even though she lacked experience. So, on her arrival, a major project was waiting on her desk.

| 19 |

It was the deep end, without a doubt, so Orpen waded in. "I'm not the sort of person who likes to be eased into things anyway," she says. It was a challenging first project but she attacked it logically and enthusiastically, and was soon travelling around the country, mixing with staff at all levels.

| 20 |

After six months of briefings, she returned to the office to find the day-to-day aspects somewhat neglected. She tore things apart and began again, putting in place solid organisational structures that would run smoothly. Orpen is proud of the fact that it functions efficiently and gets annoyed that the secretarial role is often undervalued.

| 21 |

The role doesn't always receive the recognition it deserves, she argues, despite the fact that many senior secretaries and PAs are managers in their own right. It was the management side of the PESD, in fact, that particularly interested her – she is a firm believer that today's secretaries need to be armed with the basics, at least. At her first Post Office meeting the discussion centred around Total Quality Management, and she remembers her relief at knowing what her new colleagues were talking about.

| 22 |

Orpen realises the Diploma prepared her for work in a way academic study could not. She left university with an impressive 2:1 degree in history and what she now recognises as an equally impressive ignorance of the real world.

| 23 |

In time, she would like to move into senior management, perhaps in marketing or event organisation. Studying for the Diploma has whetted her appetite for more courses and she plans to investigate a qualification in marketing. With her sights set on an MBA in a few years time, Orpen is not one to sit around. "Why stop now? You've got to have aspirations to go further, haven't you?"

A "The department was introducing a new IT initiative across the company," Orpen recalls. "My first task was to co-ordinate, organise and attend staff briefings in all the ten regions. It was terrifying."

B "The competition was tough," Orpen admits. "I didn't think I stood a chance and when the letter arrived, I thought they'd sent the wrong one." She was officially awarded her title earlier this month at a ceremony at the LCCIEB headquarters, where she was also presented with a gold medal and £200 worth of travel vouchers.

C "I could write essays until the cows came home, but I knew nothing about business." The PESD has opened doors for her, however, and she now rates it alongside her degree as an asset on which to build.

D "I love the job," she says. "It's so busy and you make so many contacts because you are in touch with staff throughout the company."

E "I'm a graduate and people often ask why I'm working as a secretary," she says. "I defend the role to the hilt, explaining that secretaries are the lifeblood of a company. It simply wouldn't function without them."

F "I couldn't believe it when I got a letter inviting me to an interview. I didn't think I stood a chance of getting such a prestigious job straight after leaving college and without having gained some experience first. I had almost not applied in the first place."

G "You need to have a grasp of management structures and theories, so you can appreciate your boss's role and get the broader picture," she says. "It helps you interpret the working environment and how you fit in."

Read the following article and then answer questions **24–29** on page **105**. On your answer sheet, indicate the letter **A**, **B**, **C** or **D** against the number of each question, **24–29**. Give only one answer to each question.

Indicate your answers **on the separate answer sheet**.

Fast Forward

"I was working so hard that I went completely crazy so now I try to do an evening class just so I am doing something which isn't work."
"I know other people who have got to where I want to be but their personal lives are a nightmare."

A survey suggests that people are working ever harder and longer. Isn't it time we learned to clock off?

Time is running out. Or so people feel. According to the latest research, forty-four per cent of British workers come home exhausted. More than half suffer from stress. By almost every measure, people are more pressured, more bothered about time – or a lack of it – than they have been for many years. Time, they feel, has been squeezed.

All over the world, the old ways of managing time are disappearing. Fixed jobs, shared rhythms of shopping, travel and leisure, and common patterns of learning, marriage, work and retirement are on the way out. Instead, the world is having to come to terms with just-in-time production and multi-tasking computers, 24-hour shopping and video-on-demand, time-share holidays and home banking. All of these are symptoms of a revolution, a transition from an industrial time culture based around fixed timetables and a clear division of labour between men who went to work and women who looked after the home, towards a new culture based around flexibility, customisation and rapid flows of information.

This new post-industrial culture offers, perhaps for the first time in history, the promise of people using time for their own needs. But far from ushering in a leisured utopia, its most immediate effect has been a growing divide between those with too much work and those without any. In top jobs, long hours have become a mark of status and success. One in eight British managers works more than sixty hours a week and more than half take home work during the week.

Part of the reason is the insecurity that has swept through so many white-collar jobs, encouraged the phenomenon of "presenteeism" rather than absenteeism – staying in the office even when there isn't any work to do. But technology has also played a part. Ubiquitous computers mean that our work will always be with us and our competitors will always be working too.

These pressures aren't confined to executives and professionals. While one in six households has no jobs at all, pressure to pay the bills and fear of redundancy mean that a quarter of all British male employees work more than forty-eight hours a week and nearly a fifth of unskilled and manual workers work more than fifty hours.

Right across the world the long decline in working hours has stopped. The use of leisure is changing too. Intensive sports like aerobics are being substituted for slower ones like golf. Families are driving round zoos rather than walking around them. And teenagers "multitask" their leisure, watching several television channels at once while also fiddling with a personal computer.

Some of the costs of this transition to a post-industrial order are all around us. Not only unemployment and overwork, high stress and high anxiety, but also less obvious ones like fatigue. But little has been done to address it head on, or to adapt institutions to a post-industrial way of life. Most institutions remain stuck in the industrial era. Within the family, even though most women now have jobs, they still do the bulk of domestic work – and consequently have fifteen hours less free time each week than men. Taken as a whole, time remains off the political agenda, treated as far less important than money or production. No political party seems to have acknowledged how much the landscape of time has changed. No one is responding to the mood that we need to find a better balance between work and life. And no one has quite come to terms with the fact that the old industrial model is being rapidly left behind.

For those seeking a better balance between work and life, there is already a marvellous institution waiting to be used. Sabbaticals offer time off to recharge the batteries, to learn a new skill or just to travel the world. At the moment, these are a rare treat for academics. With the right funding arrangements, it is not inconceivable that we could, in the future, see every seventh year taken off as a matter of course.

A previous generation of writers thought the goal was to escape from work. But this misses the point. Many people enjoy work. They find it fulfilling not only because it is a way to meet people but also because it sets goals and stretches capacities. This is surely why 78 per cent of 25–34 year-olds say that they would work even if there was no financial need.

The challenge of a post-industrial age is not to escape from work but rather to achieve more autonomy and more ways for people to control the terms on which they work, its pace and texture.

24 What is the writer's verdict on post-industrial culture?

  A People have more choice in their lives.
  B The amount of leisure time has increased.
  C It leads to bigger social divisions.
  D Everyone is obliged to work harder.

25 According to the writer, very long working hours

  A affect everyone who has a job.
  B are a problem in top jobs.
  C are found at all levels of society.
  D are mainly a result of technological change.

26 What does the writer say about political attitudes to changes in work?

  A There is a failure to address the problem.
  B The balance of work and leisure is an individual choice.
  C The old industrial model should continue to apply.
  D Changes are too expensive to implement.

27 The writer regards sabbaticals as

  A self-indulgent.
  B essential in academic work.
  C one way of improving efficiency.
  D something that all workers could have.

28 Which statement best sums up the writer's attitude to work?

  A Today's workforce demands a balance of work and leisure.
  B Financial benefits make it worthwhile.
  C It allows people to develop their potential.
  D It leads to an improved social life.

29 In the future, the writer believes that

  A there will be no escape from work.
  B workers will require greater independence.
  C politicians will try to control working practices.
  D there will be less need to make money.

Answer questions **30–49** by referring to the information four successful people give about their educational experiences on pages **107–108**.

Indicate your answers **on the separate answer sheet**.

For questions **30–49**, choose your answers from the list of people (**A–D**). Some choices may be required more than once.

Note: When more than one answer is required, these may be given **in any order**.

Who

appreciated the efforts made by his / her parents?	**30**		
had to modify an early ambition?	**31**		
was influenced in deciding what was a suitable job by his / her social origin?	**32**		
did not feel fulfilled until the start of his / her first job?	**33**		
was forced to leave college?	**34**		
benefited from not working under pressure?	**35**		
made money directly through someone else's help?	**36**		
lost an early enthusiasm for school?	**37**		
feels his / her education was of no value to his / her current work?	**38**		
had unsuccessful educational experiences after leaving school?	**39**	**40**	
wanted a job that included control of finance?	**41**		
put effort into school work?	**42**		
now assesses job applicants on criteria other than qualifications?	**43**		
completed a post-graduate qualification?	**44**		
considers their expertise comes from natural talent?	**45**	**46**	
went against the opinion of a parent?	**47**		
left school before the official school-leaving age?	**48**		
received support at college that led indirectly to a profession?	**49**		

A Peter Seldon

B Martina Cole

C Barney Edwards

D Mila Tanya Griebel

They said I was useless but look at me now

ANNE NICHOLLS meets four people who show that pleasing teachers isn't everything.

Peter Seldon, 41, is the managing director of a company producing software systems for large corporate computer networks, with a staff of about seventy.

'I had a privileged education which taught me very little. I left school at 16. Somehow, I just didn't seem to grasp things. It was a very dull period of my life: I just wasn't turned on by education. The paradox was that whilst I was not motivated to work, I didn't want to be a failure. My parents, both highly intelligent and academic, became increasingly depressed. When I went on to further education college to do three A-levels, I failed the lot. I was 19 and it really seemed to be the end of the road. I felt guilty because my parents had spent so much money on my education and made sacrifices. Fortunately, something in my brain said: 'Go into something where you can use communication skills.' So I scoured the papers and noticed that Olivetti were taking on young people to train them for sales positions. Evidently my determination came across. For the first time in my life I felt really charged up and did very well, moving on to two other companies in sales management positions. Then I started getting frustrated because I wasn't in a position to influence product strategy and had no budgetary responsibility. So I took the plunge and started up my own business with a partner and a large bank loan.

'I suppose I have a flair for selling. To some extent I think the ability to sell is innate; it's all about psychology and being persuasive. My skill is conceptualising, assessing the market and being able to recognise opportunities. I can honestly say my education is irrelevant to what I am doing now.'

Martina Cole, 33, received a £150,000 advance for her first novel, a story about a working-class woman who gets mixed up in crime in the East End of London.

'I loved primary and junior school, but as soon as I went to secondary school, I just rebelled and went downhill. I simply hated it and played truant all the time. I just found school really boring. The only thing I loved was reading. I read the whole of *The Godfather* at the age of 12 in one go. But the school didn't approve. They kept on catching me with "unsuitable" books. One of my school reports said I had outstanding ability in English, but I still got low marks for essays. "You won't amount to anything, Martina Cole," said the teachers. "You'll spend all your life just getting by on a laugh." Which is exactly what I have done.

'So I left school at 15, which was illegal, with no qualifications, got pregnant at 18, and went from job to job, working in supermarkets, offices and as a nursing auxiliary. I would often daydream about being a successful writer and was forever scribbling stories down in exercise books. But my friends said: "Working-class people like us don't do things like that. We don't write books." Then one day I jacked in my job, bought an electric typewriter with my tax rebate, said to my husband: "I'll give it a year," and set to work on my first novel. I finally sent off the manuscript to an agent and waited. And then when he told me that he'd put it up for auction with several publishers and managed to sell it for £150,000, I just couldn't believe it.

'I sometimes think that writing talent is innate, although there is a knack to it as well. I have to admit that I don't have to work at writing: the words seem to flow out of me. I am sometimes aware of my lack of knowledge of grammar and vocabulary. When I told my agent I was thinking of doing a creative writing course, he said: "Don't you dare. We can sort out the grammar. Don't ruin what you've got."'

Barney Edwards, *45, is one of Britain's leading directors of TV commercials. His company employs ten permanent staff and he has a reputation for highly creative work.*

'I always wanted to be a journalist, but wasn't very good at English language – or anything else at school for that matter. The maths teacher used to call me "MD" meaning "Mentally Deficient". The school asked me to leave because they thought I was useless. My father in desperation managed to get me a job as a trainee in the hotel business, but I couldn't stand the subservience and left. Then I started a graphics course at art college – against the wishes of my father. Unfortunately I discovered that I couldn't draw and my tutor said I had no sense of composition. The only person who gave me any encouragement was the sculpture teacher, who suggested I took photographs and told me to read anything I could lay my hands on – on reflection the best advice anyone ever gave me. But the college still kicked me out. Then I thought: "What am I going to do now?", packed my bags and came to London to try and find a job.

'That was the immense leap. After that everything was easy. I started working for a photographic agency. I worked ferociously hard. There were times I just wanted to curl up and die because I was mixing with posh photographers and I was embarrassed by my Northern accent and lack of social graces. But I also had a feeling that one day I would be noticed and had an unshakeable belief that I would be some kind of star.

'Despite my lack of academic success, I learnt three very important things: to take responsibility for my actions, to communicate well and to think both analytically and creatively. Now, when I employ someone, I don't care whether they have been to university or if they have any qualifications. I want to know what films they see, what books they read, whether they have courage, charisma, stamina and can really communicate.'

Mila Tanya Griebel, *29, is a silversmith who designs and creates Jewish ceremonial metalwork. She is building a considerable reputation.*

'At junior school, I was aware I had learning difficulties and from the age of nine I was constantly told I was stupid. This was in the days before people really understood dyslexia. At secondary school I was having to run to catch up with everyone else. In the end through sheer hard work I got onto an art foundation course and then to Middlesex Polytechnic to study for a degree in 3D design. The atmosphere at the poly was so laid back that, for the first time in my life, I was able to build up some self-confidence. At the end of my third year, my tutor suggested that I apply for an MA in silversmithing at the Royal College of Art. Those two years were the most miserable of my life and ones I look back on with loathing. You had to fit into a mould. I saw so many students emerging from tutorials in tears. I just knuckled down and worked. At the end of the year, I thought, "I'm going to fail" and was amazed when they passed me. It has taken me all of three years to build up my confidence again. But I've learnt to survive and found a niche market. Above all, I feel really passionate about what I do.'

PAPER 2   Writing (2 hours)

PART 1

1   You are secretary of an Outdoor Activities Club and have organised a one-week
    holiday in North Wales for ten members of the club who are keen on mountain-
    climbing and hill-walking. You are leaving in one week's time.

    Read the letter from the hotel you have booked and the letter from two club
    members. Then, **using the information carefully**, write the letters listed below.

… and we confirm that accommodation has been reserved for all members of
your party. We acknowledge receipt of your cheque in full and complete
settlement in advance of all charges for accommodation and meals during your
period of residence. Please note that because this is a small hotel and your party
will be occupying almost all the rooms for one week, it will not be possible to
make any refunds if any individual member of your party withdraws at the last
minute. We regard this as a block booking.

My staff and I will do our utmost to ensure that your stay with us is a pleasant
and happy one and we look forward to meeting you on Saturday.

Yours sincerely

Arthur Hughes
Manager

… Sarah and I are really sorry about this, but I'm sure that you understand
that the funeral must come first. We didn't expect to receive such sad
news. It was all totally unexpected, and now we simply can't go on holiday.
We don't feel like it and it wouldn't be right.

Do you think it would be possible for us to have our money back, or have you
already paid it to the hotel? £500 is rather a lot for us to lose. Did you
insure it? I don't suppose so – we certainly never thought of it. Could you
return our money as soon as possible?

Best wishes,

Tom and Sarah

Write appropriate **letters** to:

a) Arthur Hughes, Manager of the Dragon Hotel explaining the situation and asking
   for a refund. (approximately 125 words)
b) Tom and Sarah explaining your course of action. (approximately 125 words)

You should lay the letters out in an appropriate way but it is not necessary to include
addresses.

PART 2

Choose **one** of the following writing tasks. Your answer should follow exactly the instructions given. Write approximately 250 words.

2 You have visited a large museum in the capital city of an English speaking country. After your visit you were asked by museum staff to fill in a questionnaire. At the end of the questionnaire there is extra space to write your comments. Give your views on the presentation of the exhibits, the quality of the information available, the opportunities to buy refreshments and souvenirs and any other aspects of the museum which you feel are relevant.

Write your **comments** under suitable headings.

3 You have a pen-friend in another country to whom you have been writing in English for some years. Your friend has written to you saying that he / she is very dissatisfied with the country in which he / she is living and intends to go and live in another country. Write a letter to him / her, pointing out the advantages of staying in one's own country and the disadvantages of living abroad.

Write your **letter**.

4 You have received a letter from an English language school you once attended asking you to write an article describing your experiences there. This article is to be included in a book with other articles by students who attended the school at different times. In your article, mention the lessons, the teachers, the buildings, the social programme and anything that you have especially strong memories of.

Write your **article** for the book.

5 You have received the following memo from your boss.

MEMO

To: ...
From: Managing Director

I have received a request from the editor of an international magazine. They are going to publish a special supplement entitled 'International Job Opportunities for Young People'. He has asked me for an article about what it is like to work for our company – things like working environment, variety of work, future plans and opportunities, salary and holidays. Do you think you could write it? Be honest, but make it sound good!

Write your **article**.

English in Use (1 hour 30 minutes)

For questions **1–15**, read the text below and then decide which word best fits each space. Put the letter you choose for each question in the correct box on your answer sheet. The exercise begins with an example (**0**).

Example: | 0 | *A* | | 0 |
--- | --- | --- | ---

Food For Astronauts

It used to be thought that people could not (**0**) .... well in space, so the food (**1**) .... for astronauts consisted of bite-sized pieces of food pushed out of tubes. But now it is (**2**) .... that you can eat in space in the same way as on Earth.

The physical constraints lie in the body of the spaceship rather than the body of the astronaut. Limited storage and cooking facilities, with no space or power to (**3**) .... for complex food preparation, mean that the (**4**) .... for space nutritionists has gone beyond providing astronauts with food that is palatable and good for them. The solution has emerged in the (**5**) .... of dehydrated foods. Simply add water to the freeze-dried granules and ... bon appetit!

With space flights often (**6**) .... more than a week, astronauts cannot live on granules alone. They also take pre-cooked meals (**7**) .... in bags, which they (**8**) .... up in a small oven. These are tastier than granules but, according to Dr Helen Lane, a research nutritionist, it is difficult to get astronauts to eat as much as they need. 'It's partly that they are so busy but also because there is no (**9**) .... to eat.' So tickling their taste buds is an (**10**) .... struggle, especially since one of the effects of zero gravity is to (**11**) .... the sense of smell.

Weightlessness is an important (**12**) .... in space food because of the danger that the food might (**13**) .... and float off in different (**14**) ..... 'We need foods that coalesce,' says Dr Lane. 'Yoghurts, puddings, sauces all (**15**) .... together in large droplets. Your spoon may float away, but the food will stay on it.'

0	**A**	swallow	**B**	suck	**C**	chew	**D**	digest
1	**A**	diets	**B**	routines	**C**	programmes	**D**	agendas
2	**A**	expected	**B**	thought	**C**	revealed	**D**	known
3	**A**	provide	**B**	give	**C**	make	**D**	spare
4	**A**	opportunity	**B**	challenge	**C**	achievement	**D**	ambition
5	**A**	type	**B**	way	**C**	form	**D**	order
6	**A**	enduring	**B**	going	**C**	flying	**D**	lasting
7	**A**	sealed	**B**	tied	**C**	locked	**D**	fixed
8	**A**	cook	**B**	make	**C**	warm	**D**	serve
9	**A**	stimulation	**B**	hunger	**C**	provocation	**D**	longing
10	**A**	anxious	**B**	intense	**C**	uphill	**D**	impossible
11	**A**	control	**B**	cut	**C**	reduce	**D**	stop
12	**A**	consideration	**B**	thing	**C**	business	**D**	principle
13	**A**	break	**B**	fragment	**C**	slip	**D**	drop
14	**A**	pieces	**B**	ways	**C**	places	**D**	directions
15	**A**	maintain	**B**	link	**C**	keep	**D**	hold

For questions **16–30** complete the following article by writing each missing word in the correct box on your answer sheet. **Use only one word for each space.** The exercise begins with an example (**0**).

Example:	**0**	*one*		**0**

Chess

Chess is (**0**) .... of the world's oldest games of war. It is generally said to (**16**) .... developed in India at some period before 500 AD. The original pieces, much less mobile (**17**) .... their modern counterparts, represented units of the ancient Indian army, foot-soldiers, cavalry, armed chariots and, of course, elephants. The fighting troops (**18**) .... led on the chessboard, (**19**) .... in real life, by the king and his senior minister, the vizier, (**20**) .... became the queen in the modern game. From India, (**21**) .... is said, chess spread through China, Persia and Europe. Once the game (**22**) .... reached the West, the identity and design of the individual chess pieces was modified to reflect the social milieu of medieval Europe. The king remained unchanged but the elephant was replaced by the bishop, reflecting the power of the Church in medieval Europe. The biggest change was the emergence of the queen as the (**23**) .... powerful piece on the chessboard.

(**24**) .... the twentieth century, chess was often regarded as a game for the aristocracy of society, (**25**) .... today it exerts a much broader appeal. Among board games, chess has the ideal blend of strategy, tactics and pure skill. The only games which compare (**26**) .... subtlety, science and depth are shogi and go. The competition aspect of chess makes (**27**) .... a battle between two individuals, a battle (**28**) .... bloodshed, but still a fierce struggle of mind, will and physical endurance. More than anything (**29**) .... though, chess has an ancient and distinguished history. The game provides a deep sense of continuity with the intellectual community of past ages, extending through hundreds of years and embracing (**30**) .... nations.

In **most** lines of the following text there is **one** unnecessary word. It is either grammatically incorrect or does not fit in with the sense of the text. For each numbered line **31–46** find this word and then write it in the box on your answer sheet. Some lines are correct. Indicate these lines with a tick (✓) in the box. The exercise begins with two examples (**0**).

Examples:

0	✓		**0**
00	*they*		**0**

Marriage

0	....	A great majority of adults in the industrialised world – in fact, about 90
00	....	per cent – they will be married at some time in their lives. Of those who
31	....	do not, some may choose to remain themselves single, but others will
32	....	have no choice. An alarming number who they marry will divorce, but
33	....	this is not because marriage itself has lost its attraction – instead
34	....	people give up on particular relationships and try again. For example,
35	....	of the four out of ten American marriages that possibly end in divorce,
36	....	80 per cent are preludes to further unions. Every society has for its
37	....	own definitions of what a perfect marriage it should be. In the Western
38	....	world, it seems that a husband and wife have been a perfect marriage if
39	....	they love by each other, have no other sexual partner, display trust,
40	....	loyalty and intimacy, confide in each other, show mutual respect, are
41	....	willing to listen to their partner's concerns and are agree on their
42	....	children's upbringing. However, from a time to time the balance of
43	....	social expectations shifts. For example, a study has carried out in
44	....	1986 showed that least 74 per cent of American couples rate 'equality in
45	....	the relationship' such as an important component of marriage. We can be
46	....	fairly sure that their great-grandparents (and particularly their great-grandfathers) did not place the same value on this.

For questions **47–61** read the following two texts below. Use the words in the boxes to form **one** word that fits in the same numbered space in the text. The exercise begins with an example (**0**).

Example:

0	*cultural*	0

A LEAFLET

An Opportunity To Save Money On Books!

Fully-updated and revised for the twenty-first century, our travel guidebooks contain everything you need to know about the (**0**) .... and artistic treasures of Europe's capital cities. You will be impressed by the (**47**) .... of information they contain and by the simply stunning photographs. These books are truly (**48**) .... and are absolutely (**49**) .... for the well-informed traveller. As a special offer, prior to (**50**) .... in March, you can purchase all twenty books at the special price of £180 (normally £25 per volume), which you can pay in twelve monthly (**51**) .... of £18 if you wish. Taking one of our guidebooks with you (**52**) .... that you are fully-informed about each city that you visit. Think of it as an (**53**) .... in your holidays for years to come.

(0)	CULTURE
(47)	DEEP
(48)	STAND
(49)	DISPENSE
(50)	PUBLISH
(51)	INSTALL
(52)	SURE
(53)	INVEST

A NEWSLETTER

Changes In The High Street

In the last newsletter we reported plans to relocate the bus stops and change parking (**54**) .... in the High Street. This work has now been completed but there have been many (**55**) .... from shopkeepers and local (**56**) .... The (**57**) .... of the changes was to make it easier for buses to re-enter the stream of traffic and to increase the number of car parking spaces. (**58**) .... , there have been several (**59**) .... as cars reverse into the traffic from the area where the buses used to stop. Also, the old bus stops are still in position so people who are unaware of the changes still stand there, and express (**60**) .... when the bus does not stop. Next Tuesday evening there will be a public meeting at which people can make suggestions for (**61**) .... to the situation.

(54)	ARRANGE
(55)	COMPLAIN
(56)	RESIDE
(57)	INTEND
(58)	FORTUNE
(59)	COLLIDE
(60)	ANNOY
(61)	IMPROVE

For questions **62–74**, read the following advertisement and use the information in it to complete the numbered gaps in the memo. Then write the new words in the correct boxes on your answer sheet. **Use no more than two words** for each gap. The words you need **do not occur** in the advertisement. The exercise begins with an example (**0**).

Example:

0	*the market*	0

Bolingbroke House   Grade II Listed Building
Newly Offered

FOR SALE

Suitable for use as Hotel, Private School, Health Farm, Conference Centre.

Designed by the renowned architect, Sir John Vanburgh in the early 18th century, this elegant building possesses the architectural features of a bygone age. Victorian additions almost doubled the size of the house. Fully restored, refurbished and modernised, it is offered for immediate use.

- 85 rooms   • Room for further expansion   • Large car parking area
- Set in 3,000 hectares of well-maintained gardens and parkland
- Cinema, lecture hall, seminar rooms, closed-circuit television, public address system
- Indoor swimming pool, gymnasium, tennis courts
- Dining hall, modern kitchens   • Modern security systems

60 kilometres from central London, local station 2 km
25 km Heathrow Airport   Well-placed for motorway connections
Guide price: £2,500,000

MEMO

To: Sir John Hawkwood   *Date:* 16 June
From: Thomas Middleton   *Re:*   Conference Centre

Our company has been in need of its own centre for conferences and training courses for some time. I believe that I have now found the ideal location. It is a Grade II listed building which has just come onto
(**0**) .... It was designed by Sir John Vanburgh. The main house
(**62**) .... to the early eighteenth century but (**63**) .... the present building (**64**) ....Victorian times. There is (**65**) .... for the company to spend more money on improving the house as it is offered in
(**66**) .... There are (**67**) .... a hundred rooms, with
(**68**) .... of adding more. There is (**69**) .... space to park cars. A considerable amount of (**70**) .... is included in the price. Obviously, the house has the appropriate rooms and (**71**) .... needed for conferences. In addition, members of staff attending conferences will be able to
(**72**) .... by taking advantage of the many opportunities for physical exercise that are available.

The house is (**73**) .... against intruders. It is also easy to get to from central London and Heathrow Airport, both by rail and by road. The price is £2,500,000 but there may be room for (**74**) ....

For questions **75–80**, read through the following text and then choose from the list **A–J** below the best phrase to fill each of the spaces. Write one letter (**A–J**) in the correct box on your answer sheet. **Some of the suggested answers do not fit at all.** The exercise begins with an example (**0**).

Example: 0   *J*   0 ▭ ▮

The Pull of the Land

MOTORISTS driving along Croy Brae in Strathclyde, Scotland, sooner or later slow down or stop completely in utter confusion. For Croy Brae is one of the most disorienting places on earth. Approaching the brae ('hill') from the north is an uncanny experience. (**0**) .... and drivers assume that the slope will accelerate the vehicle. Yet if they slow down, they are likely to come to a complete halt. (**75**) .... , the road runs uphill, not downhill. Unable to believe what has happened, many motorists stop, only to find that their car begins to slide backwards, 'uphill'. (**76**) .... but in reverse. Thinking they are heading uphill, they accelerate, only to discover that they are speeding along faster than they intended. The road actually goes down.

No one has yet been able to come up with a satisfactory explanation of what causes these strange effects at Croy Brae. (**77**) .... magnetic forces induced by the surrounding iron-rich rocks exerted such a strong attraction that they could actually pull automobiles uphill. (**78**) .... , but another theory suggests that the sensations are due to an optical illusion caused by local variations in the earth's magnetic field – to which our sense of balance may somehow be linked. (**79**) .... the phenomenon is not unique to Croy; there are similar places all over the world. Such roads have to be driven to be believed. (**80**) .... can ever be explained, such conjuring tricks of nature are a magnet for tourists and all lovers of the strange and bizarre.

A   Whether or not the truth about them
B   Despite every appearance to the contrary
C   This explanation is now generally dismissed
D   People on foot have similar experiences
E   Whatever the explanation
F   Little that is known about this experience
G   Travellers who are approaching from the south experience a similar situation
H   People do not realise
I   It was once believed that

J   The road appears to slope downwards

PART 1

You will hear someone talking about the developments of the telephone. For questions **1–10**, fill in the missing information.

You will hear the recording twice.

The History Of The Telephone

Cost of a phone in 1880: _____ **1**

What this cost represented for an average working man:

_____ **2**

Before 1920's, most phones were found:

_____ **3**

Three changes in 1920's: _____ **4**

_____ **5**

_____ **6**

Most calls then routed: _____ **7**

Last manual exchange closed: _____ **8**

Disadvantages of old system in emergency:

_____ **9**

_____ **10**

You will hear an answerphone message announcing details of rail and steam attractions at the weekend. For questions **11–20**, complete the information sheet according to the information you hear.

Listen very carefully as you will hear the recording ONCE only.

Weekend Attractions

Attractions at Swanley:

train ride

	11

	12

	13

Attractions at _____ 14

travel to Henderson Island by _____ 15

visit village built like something in _____ 16

one departure at _____ 17

Attractions at Matlock:

3 types of tram:

	18

steam

	19

children free if they bring a _____ 20

You will hear a radio interview with a person who is blind. For questions **21–28**, choose the most suitable answers (**A**, **B**, **C** or **D**).

You will hear the recording twice.

21   What does James Powell's understanding of the visual world come from?
   A   The visual concept acquired before going blind.
   B   His sense of spatial awareness.
   C   His knowledge of how other people behave.
   D   His understanding of the way people react to him.

22   A major problem for blind people, in James's opinion, is how to
   A   get round and about.
   B   interact effectively with other people.
   C   recognise when they are being addressed.
   D   conduct a conversation.

23   James wants to dispel the misconception that blind people
   A   develop their sense of hearing to compensate for not seeing.
   B   don't know what's going on when in large groups of people.
   C   rely on a sharp sense of where objects are placed.
   D   are unaware of light and colour.

24   To help sighted people in their attitude towards the blind, how does James behave?
   A   He talks about the difficulties he encounters.
   B   He behaves naturally in all situations.
   C   He tries not to overreact in stressful situations.
   D   He never draws attention to his disability.

25   What is James's view of the education he received?
   A   constructive
   B   bitter
   C   accepting
   D   dismissive

26   James went to a school where
   A   sighted and non-sighted were taught together.
   B   the blind children spent part of the day doing special lessons apart from the other pupils.
   C   all the children had some disability.
   D   the disabled children had separate lessons but joined the other children for certain activities.

27   What is James's job?
   A   He's a computer programmer.
   B   He's a writer.
   C   He trains people to use computers.
   D   He trains people to teach those who are blind.

28   As James gets older, he
   A   gets satisfaction from different areas of his life.
   B   finds it easier to cope with his disability.
   C   improves his skills in some areas.
   D   sees that he needs an emotional escape.

You will hear **five** short extracts in which different people talk about performing in public.

Performing in Public

TASK ONE

For questions **29–33**, match the extracts as you hear them with the people, listed **A–H**.

A   trumpeter

B   pianist

	29

C   lawyer

	30

D   singer

	31

E   newsreader

	32

F   drummer

	33

G   actor

H   psychologist

TASK TWO

For questions **34–38**, match the extracts as you hear them with the actions, listed **A–H**.

A   had an understanding with other people about how to behave

B   tried to solve the situation by using pills

	34

C   had a problem consulting notes

	35

D   had prepared well in advance

	36

E   compared a personal situation with that of other people

	37

F   gave a general explanation of the problem

	38

G   suffered from a dry throat

H   stopped in the middle of the performance

Remember that you must complete both tasks as you listen. You will hear the recording twice.

PAPER 5   Speaking (15 minutes)

Answer these questions:

What kind of spare time activities do you enjoy?
Do you prefer sports or non-sporting activities?
How much of your spare time do you like to spend by yourself?
In what ways have your spare time activities changed compared with a few years ago?
How have your leisure activities been influenced by technology?

PART 2   (3 or 4 minutes)

Past and Present (Compare, contrast and speculate)

Turn to pictures 1–2 on page 141 which show the same town about a hundred years ago and now.

Candidate A, describe the changes that have taken place and suggest reasons for the changes. What changes will take place in the next hundred years? You have a minute to do this.

Candidate B, what changes do you think will happen in the future?

Before and After (Compare, contrast and speculate)

Turn to pictures 1–2 on page 142 which show the same place at different times.

Candidate B, describe the changes that have taken place, saying what you think has caused them. You have a minute to do this.

Candidate A, what do you think will happen next in this place?

PART 3   (3 or 4 minutes)

Student Appeal (Discuss, speculate and select)

Turn to pictures 1–5 on page 143. A college is considering how to make itself more attractive to students. Here are pictures of some of the things it is considering. Which two do you think would be most successful in attracting students?

PART 4   (3 or 4 minutes)

Answer these questions:

Did you reach agreement?
How do your opinions differ?
Are there any other things that attract you to a particular college?
What is it that you find really unattractive about a college?
What improvements would you suggest for your present college?

Answer Sheets

Papers 1, 3 and 4 all have answer sheets.

- You can make notes on your question paper, but you must transfer your answers to the answer sheet. Notes on the question paper won't be marked.

- Leave enough time (10–15 minutes) to transfer your answers to the answer sheets.

PAPER 1   Multiple Choice Answer Sheet

- Use a pencil to shade in the lozenges, and a rubber to correct mistakes.

- Record your answers carefully. Check that only one lozenge is shaded on each line. Make sure that your shaded lozenge corresponds to the correct question number.

PAPER 3   Answer Sheets

- Do not write more words than a question specifies. If a question asks for two words in each gap, write two words. If you write three, no marks will be awarded.

- Make sure you use correct spelling.

PAPER 4   Listening Comprehension Answer Sheet

- Answers will usually be between one and three words.

- You will have time at the end of the exam to transfer your answers to your answer sheet.

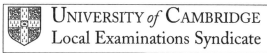

UNIVERSITY of CAMBRIDGE
Local Examinations Syndicate

SAMPLE

Candidate Name
If not already printed, write name
in CAPITALS and complete the
Candidate No. grid (in pencil).

Candidate's signature

Examination Title

Centre

Supervisor:

☒ If the candidate is ABSENT or has WITHDRAWN shade here ▭

Centre No.

Candidate No.

Examination Details

0	0	0	0
1	1	1	1
2	2	2	2
3	3	3	3
4	4	4	4
5	5	5	5
6	6	6	6
7	7	7	7
8	8	8	8
9	9	9	9

Multiple-choice Answer Sheet

Use a pencil   Mark one letter for each question.

For example:

If you think C is the right answer to the
question, mark your answer sheet like this:

Change your answer
like this:

1	A B C D E F G H I	21	A B C D E F G H I	41	A B C D E F G H I
2	A B C D E F G H I	22	A B C D E F G H I	42	A B C D E F G H I
3	A B C D E F G H I	23	A B C D E F G H I	43	A B C D E F G H I
4	A B C D E F G H I	24	A B C D E F G H I	44	A B C D E F G H I
5	A B C D E F G H I	25	A B C D E F G H I	45	A B C D E F G H I
6	A B C D E F G H I	26	A B C D E F G H I	46	A B C D E F G H I
7	A B C D E F G H I	27	A B C D E F G H I	47	A B C D E F G H I
8	A B C D E F G H I	28	A B C D E F G H I	48	A B C D E F G H I
9	A B C D E F G H I	29	A B C D E F G H I	49	A B C D E F G H I
10	A B C D E F G H I	30	A B C D E F G H I	50	A B C D E F G H I
11	A B C D E F G H I	31	A B C D E F G H I	51	A B C D E F G H I
12	A B C D E F G H I	32	A B C D E F G H I	52	A B C D E F G H I
13	A B C D E F G H I	33	A B C D E F G H I	53	A B C D E F G H I
14	A B C D E F G H I	34	A B C D E F G H I	54	A B C D E F G H I
15	A B C D E F G H I	35	A B C D E F G H I	55	A B C D E F G H I
16	A B C D E F G H I	36	A B C D E F G H I	56	A B C D E F G H I
17	A B C D E F G H I	37	A B C D E F G H I	57	A B C D E F G H I
18	A B C D E F G H I	38	A B C D E F G H I	58	A B C D E F G H I
19	A B C D E F G H I	39	A B C D E F G H I	59	A B C D E F G H I
20	A B C D E F G H I	40	A B C D E F G H I	60	A B C D E F G H I

CAE1

DP306/80

UNIVERSITY of CAMBRIDGE
Local Examinations Syndicate

SAMPLE

Candidate Name
If not already printed, write name
in CAPITALS and complete the
Candidate No. grid (in pencil).

Candidate's signature

Examination Title

Centre

Supervisor:

[X] If the candidate is ABSENT or has WITHDRAWN shade here ⬜

Centre No.

Candidate No.

Examination Details

0	0	0	0
1	1	1	1
2	2	2	2
3	3	3	3
4	4	4	4
5	5	5	5
6	6	6	6
7	7	7	7
8	8	8	8
9	9	9	9

Candidate Answer Sheet

Use a pencil

For **Parts 1** and **6**:
Mark ONE letter for each question.
For example, if you think **B** is the
right answer to the question,
mark your answer sheet like this:

0 ⬜A̲ ⬛B̲ ⬜C̲ ⬜D̲

For **Parts 2, 3, 4** and **5**:
Write your answers in the spaces
next to the numbers like this:

0 | *example*

Part 1				
1	A	B	C	D
2	A	B	C	D
3	A	B	C	D
4	A	B	C	D
5	A	B	C	D
6	A	B	C	D
7	A	B	C	D
8	A	B	C	D
9	A	B	C	D
10	A	B	C	D
11	A	B	C	D
12	A	B	C	D
13	A	B	C	D
14	A	B	C	D
15	A	B	C	D

Part 2	Do not write here
16	16
17	17
18	18
19	19
20	20
21	21
22	22
23	23
24	24
25	25
26	26
27	27
28	28
29	29
30	30

Turn over for parts 3 - 6 →

CAE-3

DP394/338

SAMPLE

Part 3		Do not write here
31		31
32		
33		33
34		34
35		35
36		36
37		37
38		38
39		39
40		40
41		41
42		42
43		43
44		44
45		45
46		46

Part 4		Do not write here
47		47
48		48
49		49
50		50
51		51
52		52
53		53
54		54
55		55
56		56
57		57
58		58
59		59
60		60
61		61

Part 5		Do not write here
62		62
63		63
64		64
65		65
66		66
67		67
68		68
69		69
70		70
71		71
72		72
73		73
74		74

Part 6									
75	A	B	C	D	E	F	G	H	I
76	A	B	C	D	E	F	G	H	I
77	A	B	C	D	E	F	G	H	I
78	A	B	C	D	E	F	G	H	I
79	A	B	C	D	E	F	G	H	I
80	A	B	C	D	E	F	G	H	I

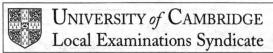

UNIVERSITY *of* CAMBRIDGE
Local Examinations Syndicate

SAMPLE

Candidate Name
If not already printed, write name
in CAPITALS and complete the
Candidate No. grid (in pencil).
Candidate's signature

Examination Title

Centre

Supervisor:
[X] If the candidate is ABSENT or has WITHDRAWN shade here ▭

Centre No.

Candidate No.

Examination Details

0	0	0	0
1	1	1	1
2	2	2	2
3	3	3	3
4	4	4	4
5	5	5	5
6	6	6	6
7	7	7	7
8	8	8	8
9	9	9	9

Listening Comprehension Answer Sheet

Enter the test number here ▢▢▢

For office use only ⊏3⊐ CPE   ⊏5⊐ CAE   ⊏0⊐⊏1⊐⊏2⊐⊏3⊐⊏4⊐⊏5⊐⊏6⊐⊏7⊐⊏8⊐⊏9⊐
⊏0⊐⊏1⊐⊏2⊐⊏3⊐⊏4⊐⊏5⊐⊏6⊐⊏7⊐⊏8⊐⊏9⊐

Write your answers below	Do not write here	Continue here	Do not write here
1	▭ 1 ▭	**21**	▭ 21 ▭
2	▭ 2 ▭	**22**	▭ 22 ▭
3	▭ 3 ▭	**23**	▭ 23 ▭
4	▭ 4 ▭	**24**	▭ 24 ▭
5	▭ 5 ▭	**25**	▭ 25 ▭
6	▭ 6 ▭	**26**	▭ 26 ▭
7	▭ 7 ▭	**27**	▭ 27 ▭
8	▭ 8 ▭	**28**	▭ 28 ▭
9	▭ 9 ▭	**29**	▭ 29 ▭
10	▭ 10 ▭	**30**	▭ 30 ▭
11	▭ 11 ▭	**31**	▭ 31 ▭
12	▭ 12 ▭	**32**	▭ 32 ▭
13	▭ 13 ▭	**33**	▭ 33 ▭
14	▭ 14 ▭	**34**	▭ 34 ▭
15	▭ 15 ▭	**35**	▭ 35 ▭
16	▭ 16 ▭	**36**	▭ 36 ▭
17	▭ 17 ▭	**37**	▭ 37 ▭
18	▭ 18 ▭	**38**	▭ 38 ▭
19	▭ 19 ▭	**39**	▭ 39 ▭
20	▭ 20 ▭	**40**	▭ 40 ▭

Visuals for Paper 5

Candidate A

Candidate B

VISUALS FOR PAPER 5

Candidates A and B

Candidate A

VISUALS FOR PAPER 5

Candidate B

Candidates A and B

Candidate A

Candidate B

Candidates A and B

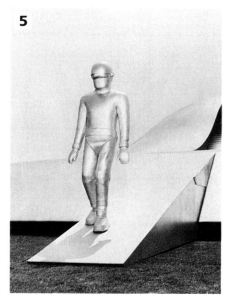

Candidate A

VISUALS FOR PAPER 5

Candidate B

1

2

3

4

5

Candidates A and B

Candidate A

Candidate B

Candidates A and B

Smaller classes

Better computer facilities

Bigger and better library

Better and cheaper food

A good social programme

CAMBRIDGE LEVEL 5

CPE

Fully operational command of the spoken language.

Able to handle communication in most situations, including unfamiliar or unexpected ones.

Able to use accurate and appropriate linguistic resources to express complex ideas and concepts and produce extended discourse that is coherent and always easy to follow.

Rarely produces inaccuracies and inappropriacies.

Pronunciation is easily understood and prosodic features are used effectively; many features including pausing and hesitation are 'native-like'.

CAMBRIDGE LEVEL 4

CAE

Good operational command of the spoken language.

Able to handle communication in most situations.

Able to use accurate and appropriate linguistic resources to express ideas and produce discourse that is generally coherent.

Occasionally produces inaccuracies and inappropriacies.

Maintains a flow of language with only natural hesitation resulting from considerations of appropriacy or expression.

L1 accent may be evident but does not affect the clarity of the message.

CAMBRIDGE LEVEL 3

FCE

Generally effective command of the spoken language.

Able to handle communication in familiar situations.

Able to organise extended discourse but occasionally produces utterances that lack coherence and some inaccuracies and inappropriate usage occur.

Maintains a flow of language, although hesitation may occur whilst searching for language resources.

Although pronunciation is easily understood, L1 features may be intrusive.

Does not require major assistance or prompting by an interlocutor.

CAMBRIDGE LEVEL 2 (Threshold)

PET

Limited but effective command of the spoken language.

Able to handle communication in most familiar situations.

Able to construct longer utterances but is not able to use complex language except in well-rehearsed utterances.

Has problems searching for language resources to express ideas and concepts resulting in pauses and hesitation.

Pronunciation is generally intelligle, but L1 features may put a strain on the listener.

Has some ability to compensate for communication difficulties using repair strategies but may require prompting and assistance by an interlocutor.

CAMBRIDGE LEVEL 1 (Waystage)

KET

Basic command of the spoken language.

Able to convey basic meaning in very familiar or highly predictable situations.

Produces utterances which tend to be very short – words or phrases – with frequent hesitations and pauses.

Dependent on rehearsed or formulaic phrases with limited generative capacity.

Only able to produce limited extended discourse.

Pronunciation is heavily influenced by L1 features and may at times be difficult to understand.

Requires prompting and assistance by an interlocutor to prevent communication from breaking down.

Pre-Waystage Level

Zero

Extract from CAE Handbook ©UCLES 1999

Key

Test 1

Part 1: Rites Of Passage

1   B: After working for nine months as a guitar technician …
2   A: full-time employment has not brought the deluge of cash … He is still seeking a permanent position.
3   B: Lack of money meant he was forced back home.
4/5 C: "I got a bit depressed … there was a lot of camaraderie on my course".
4/5 D: Kelly Moore was going through similar emotions.
6   E: Rebecca Jones is looking forward to leaving college …
7   B: Mike … start(ed) his own business.
8   E: Not all students are daunted by … the jobs market. Rebecca Jones …
9   A: and the office politics are a nightmare …
10 E: She will take "any job going" to pay off her debts.
11 D: I was offered a job … on the day I graduated.
12 D: It taught me self-discipline, how to organise myself …

Total = 12 marks

Part 2: A Consuming Addiction

13 G: Link between 'a 75 per cent rise in disposable income' and 'Having more money'.
14 C: Link between 'Her research' and introduction of Dr Dittmar.
15 E: Links between 'how shoppers feel about themselves' and 'poor self-image'.
16 A: Links between 'bought on impulse' and 'impulsive purchases'.
17 F: Links between 'was found', 'This finding' and references to regret.
18 D: Links between 'advertisers and retailers' and 'advertisements and shopping environments.'

Total = 12 marks

Part 3: Heroes And Villains

19 C: Correct. The key word is 'unlike'. The first paragraph says 'But almost all end up doing one or the other … There never seems to be time to do both properly. But William Carlos Williams … succeeded.'
19 A, B, D: Incorrect. They are all true but do not answer the question.
20 B: Correct. 'His "Doctor Stories" deal with crises understood by any contemporary inner-city GP …' (para. 3)

20 A: Incorrect. They were not typical of the time, but rather of the place.
20 C: Incorrect. The writer says the same problems exist today 'still birth, autopsy …'.
20 D: Incorrect. It is specific to a 'working class industrial township' or 'inner city', not a region (= New Jersey).
21 D: Correct. 'My visits are made to the concrete tower block of Tower Hamlets … and the new immigrants are from Vietnam and Bangladesh.' (para. 3)
21 A: Incorrect. The writer likes Williams's poetry but does not mention the poet's literary tastes.
21 B: Incorrect. He refers to his own feelings – 'disgruntled', and to Williams's characteristics – 'how to listen …' – but does not say that they have the same temperament.
21 C: Incorrect. The writer only mentions Williams's family background.
22 D: Correct. 'on his laboratory typewriter … "By the time we assembled for breakfast"'. (para. 4)
22 A: Incorrect. Only 'night-visiting' of patients is mentioned.
22 B: Incorrect. The text does not say when he held his surgeries.
22 C: Incorrect. There is no reference to afternoon activities.
23 B: Correct. 'still woefully underrated body of work.' (para. 6)
23 A: Incorrect. He does not say that his high opinion is shared by others.
23 C: Incorrect. He does not compare Williams's past and present reputation but only expresses his personal opinion.
23 D: Incorrect. The writer does not refer to other poets.
24 B: Correct. 'whenever I become disgruntled about the workload'. (para. 6)
24 A: Incorrect. 'crises understood by any contemporary inner-city GP' (para. 3) and the following examples shows that the writer finds his own work challenging.
24 C: Incorrect. The writer speculates on Williams's motivation in paragraphs 2 and 7 but does not discuss his own.
24 D: Incorrect. He mentions the problem of writing and practising medicine only in general terms.

Total = 12 marks

Part 4: An English Family, 80 Years Of Schooling

25 B: Everyone worked locally. (para. 3)
26 C: Mike Brett mentioned early failure and says he is a 'late developer'. (para. 5)
27 A: there were not the chances there are now. (para. 1)
28 D: I was an outcast among my own kind: virtually ostracised. (para. 3)
29 A: Only two people went on to secondary education in my time. (para. 1)
30 A: We learned to add up in our heads. (para. 1)
31 B: Only one place each year went to someone from my school, and I got it. (para. 3)

32 B: My parents had to make a great financial sacrifice …
(para. 3)

33 D: I couldn't do what I wanted to do … . They (the school)
wouldn't let me … (para. 10)

34 C: So I went to the secondary modern … / We moved, and
I applied for a place at Felixstowe Grammar School.
(para. 7)
Note that the question refers to 'secondary school'.
Freda Brett also went to different schools but not
secondary ones.

35 D: Most of my teachers made particular emphasis that boys
and girls are equal. (para. 9)
For a question like this apply your knowledge of the
world. It is more likely to refer to a teacher now than
one in the past.

36 C: One of my economics teachers was quite different from
other teachers I'd had. (para. 7)

37 B: 'there was … always the threat of being expelled' refers
to the idea of 'expulsion'. (para. 4)

38 C: The school wouldn't support my going to university …
But then the A level examination results came out, the
school changed its mind … (para. 8)

39 D: We had penpals … who we communicated with by
computer. (para. 9)
Common sense should indicate the best place to look
for a reference to technology.

40 C: Mike Brett refers to a school exam 'but I failed anyway'
(para. 5). We know it was important because he had a
private tutor.

41 C: And by then I knew I wanted to teach. (para. 6)

42 D: I'm having to do an extra evening class in music …
(para. 10)
Note that this question does not refer to Mike Brett
because his private tutor is not linked with a subject.

Total = 18 marks

PAPER 2   Writing

Part 1

Question 1

Style: Formal letter. Begin 'Dear Mr. Wolff' and end 'Yours
sincerely'. Use full forms and avoid informal phrasal verbs
and expressions.

Content: Your main points must be taken from the annotations
on the letter. These are:
1 delay in replying
2 reckless self-exposure to danger not applicable in this
case
3 inadequate sum / surprising exchange rate

Part 2

Question 2

Style: Use a headline, sub-headings and a fairly colloquial style.

Content: Mention two or three restaurants. Name them and say
where they are.
Say something about the quality of cooking, the

pleasant atmosphere, value for money.
Mention additional points of your own.
Be complimentary. You are not asked to criticise the
restaurants.

Question 3

Style: Use a report format. You may number the paragraphs or
give them headings.

Content: Mention examples of untidiness, lack of cleanliness,
need for repair and suggest solutions in each case. Say
which problems must be dealt with first.

Question 4

Style: Informal and colloquial. Use headings and sub-headings.

Content: Mention pleasures, problems, equipment and cost.

Question 5

Style: Formal letter. Begin 'Dear Sir or Madam' and end 'Yours
faithfully'.

Content: Mention the job you are applying for and where you
saw the advertisement.
Describe your educational qualifications and your
previous experience.
Provide evidence that you have the three abilities
mentioned in the advertisement.
Say when you are available for interview.

PAPER 3   English in Use

There is 1 mark for each correct answer in Parts 1–6.

Part 1: History Set In Stone

1 D: 'bones' and 'parts' do not collocate with 'plant',
although they do go with 'animal'. 'Evidence' does not
collocate with either.

2 B: 'paw' refers to animals and can make a print.

3 B: The idea is that there is still something to see.

4 D: The meaning is negative – 'trace' is the weakest word.

5 A: 'name' collocates with 'give' and 'palaeontology' is the
name of a science.

6 A: The implied contrast is with 'dead'.

7 A: The idea is that we can easily find this type.

8 C: We need a word that describes their appearance.

9 D: The idea is 'turned to stone'. This is a fixed collocation.

10 D: This is the set phrase for what you see in museums,
zoos, etc.

11 A: This word collocates with 'to extinction'.

12 A: 'Connect ideas' is the implied collocation.

13 A: Only 'climatic' has a long-term, permanent meaning.

14 B: The idea is moving something from one place to
another.

15 B: Only B collocates with 'of sunlight'.

Total = 15 marks

Part 2: Language Variety

16 *within* (preposition): meaning 'not more than'.

17 *there* (adverb): this goes with 'has not been'.

18 *much / strong / such (determiner):* refers to the regional variation already mentioned.

19 *all (part of adverbial phrase):* meaning 'it is impossible'.

20 *ever (adverb):* meaning 'at any time in the future'.

21 *what (relative pronoun):* referring to 'transport and communication conditions'.

22 *even (adverb):* emphasising the contrast with 1,500.

23 *though (conjunction):* collocates with 'even'.

24 *a (indefinite article):* a possibility, not something that exists.

25 *did (auxiliary verb):* refers to 'break up'.

26 *longer (part of adverbial phrase):* collocates with 'no' referring to time.

27 *this (demonstrative):* refers to breaking up into unintelligible languages.

28 *least (part of adverbial phrase):* collocates with 'at'.

29 *will (auxiliary verb):* reference is clearly to the future.

30 *as (conjunction):* 'as to' refers to a possible result.

Total = 15 marks

Part 3: Insincerity

31 *up (particle):* 'Make up' doesn't make sense because it means 'to invent'. The key phrase is 'make comparisons'.

32 *the (definite article):* If 'the' occurs twice in one line it is not the word you are looking for.

33 *those (determiner):* 'Generations' have not been previously mentioned so 'those' is unnecessary.

34 *such (modifier):* 'such' refers back to something. There is no previous mention of 'insincere remarks and flattery'.

35 ✓

36 *with (preposition):* 'mating' is an adjective describing 'partners'.

37 *unique (adjective):* The text refers to 'animal deception', so this is not a unique human talent.

38 ✓

39 *sharp (adjective):* This changes the meaning of 'thinking' in an inappropriate way.

40 *of (preposition):* Just a noun is needed after 'many' unless it is 'many of the occasions …'

41 *themselves (pronoun):* 'avoid' is not a reflexive verb.

42 ✓

43 *have (auxiliary verb):* 'tend' is an infinitive not a past participle.

44 ✓

45 *some (quantifier):* There is no need to limit 'future attempts'.

46 *is (verb):* 'as with' is a fixed comparative phrase.

Total = 16 marks

Part 4: Application Details

47 *responsibility (adjective to noun)*

48 *recruitment (verb to noun)*

49 *commercial (noun to adjective)*

50 *representatives (verb to plural noun)*

51 *enable (adjective to verb)*

52 *procedures (verb to plural noun)*

53 *unsuccessful (noun to adjective plus negative prefix):* A negative is necessary for the sentence to make sense.

A Job In The Theatre

54 *energetic (noun to adjective)*

55 *publicity (adjective to noun)*

56 *financial (noun to adjective)*

57 *satisfying (verb to adjective)*

58 *annually (adjective to adverb)*

59 *arrangements (verb to plural noun)*

60 *refunded (noun to verb):* Note that a prefix is needed here.

61 *performance (verb to noun)*

Total = 15 marks

Part 5: Titan Agricultural Products

62 *attended:* Everyone turned up …

63 *dissatisfaction:* (people) complained … . 'Dissatisfaction' goes with 'expressed'.

64 *samples / products:* stuff. 'Samples / products' are more formal words.

65 *agreement:* all reps … . They all had the same opinion, so their agreement was complete.

66 *effective:* worse than useless … . The memo has the word 'not …' so we need a positive word to go with it.

67 *point / complaint:* The key word in the letter is 'Also'. The reps are making a number of points. The answer has to collocate with 'made'.

68 *to contact:* Get through.

69 *evening:* after six.

70 *deserted / closed / empty:* everybody had gone home.

71 *informed them / notified them:* The reps are complaining that nobody lets them know about things.

72 *unaware / ignorant:* kept in the dark.

73 *to investigate:* look into.

74 *a future / a later / the next:* see them again.

Total = 13 marks

Part 6: Staying Healthy In Space

75 C: The sentence begins with 'If' and has the grammar of a zero conditional sentence. The present simple tense is used in both clauses.

76 B: The first part of the sentence says 'begin'. B refers to a contrasting later time: 'after even a week.'

77 A: 77 D looks correct because of the repetition of 'known' but consider the meaning. It means that scientists will never discover something about the human body (D says 'will' not 'may'). This does not seem likely. If scientists do not know something, they must be asking questions.

78 H: Astronauts are weightless in space – space suits make them heavy enough to walk normally.

79 F: Links between 'the limit of …' and 'two years' in the following sentences, which link with 'long flights'.

80 G: 'Mankind's dream of visiting other planets' is the subject of this clause so a verb must follow. 'Reality' contrasts with 'dream'.

Total = 6 marks

PAPER 4 · Listening

There is 1 mark for each correct answer in Parts 1–4.

Part 1: Course Information

1 *Art in Italy:* … course A753 on Art in Italy.
2 *handout:* if anyone who should be here is not, then I'll be able to put … the handouts.
3 *mail / post:* in the post.
4 *TMAs (tutor-marked assignments) / work assessment:* the first is how their work is going to be assessed … TMAs as we call them.
5 *four:* to supply four pieces of written work.
6 *late:* essential you submit your assignment by the required date.
7 *a guide:* Word length … You can regard this as a guide.
8 *typed:* we always prefer assignments to be typed.
9 *(written / separate) report:* You'll also be receiving a separately written report.
10 *a bibliography / a list of books used:* include all your sources of information.

Total = 10 marks

Part 2: Travel News

11 *derailment:* more news about the derailment.
12 *6.55:* to be precise at six fifty-five a.m.
13 *goods:* a goods train came off the track.
14 *Wales – London (Paddington):* this has blocked the main line from Wales to London.
15 *None:* no one has been killed or injured.
16 *fallen tree:* the accident was … caused … by a fallen tree.
17 *(very) late:* trains from cities in South Wales … will be subject to heavy delay.
18 *(as) normal / OK:* Trains from Gloucester to Swindon are not affected …
19 *on time:* Passengers travelling from … Bath … to London Paddington should therefore experience no delays.
20 *(much) longer:* trains to Wales … will take an alternative, and much longer, route … This will result in considerably increased journey times …

Total = 10 marks

Part 3: Actresses At Work

21 *younger:* … and play younger roles.
22 *the Actor's Union:* was asked by the Actor's Union to investigate.
23 *theatre:* I looked at people in the theatre, on TV and radio.
24 *television.*
25 *radio.*
(23–25 in any order)
26 *earnings / pay:* and earnings … Another important thing is pay.
27 *in their forties:* the busiest time is when they're in their forties.
28 *experience:* the rates of pay … are based on experience.

29 *writers:* they blame the writers.
30 *women:* there's a 55–45 per cent ratio of women to men listening in the afternoon.

Total = 10 marks

Part 4: Losing Your Job

31 B: my typing … the executives didn't need so much back-up.
32 D: you are going to feel up and down – that's quite normal.
33 G: didn't seem to want to spend so much on promoting their products.
34 F: my company – we're always on the look-out for people.
35 A: long-running serial … in front of the cameras.
36 B: I've had to re-schedule payments to the bank.
37 C: Make sure you structure your day.
38 D: redundancy money, but he said, no, there wouldn't be any.
39 A: people who've seen redundancy as a positive step.
40 G: the show came off within a month.

Total = 10 marks

PAPER 5   Speaking

Part 1

I always travel to college on foot / by bus / car / train.
I think it generally works well but it could be improved by …
There are some aspects of it which are really inconvenient.
I much prefer travelling by … / What I like best is travelling by …

Test 2

PAPER 1   Reading

Part 1: They Think It's All Over

1 B: He tells of driving his car … and would crash into me.
2 E: to prepare players for the outside world … Brendan Batson of the PFA.
3 A: Retirement was never a problem for Stan Bowles.
4 A: Morgan was silent.
5 B: Marsh was outwardly prepared for the transition.
6 D: Bruno lost his temper at home … a court order against him.
7 C: Latchford ran a childrenswear business … worked for a company … got back into the game.
8 D: The anger in Frank Bruno's eyes … I went into self-destruct.
9 F: and felt like a stranger.
10 E: they are … having to start at the bottom rung.
11 E: Batson's own career was ended at 31 by injury.

12 D: My trainer once warned me … and he was right.
13 D: it was like a bereavement.
14 F: he drove for Jaguar … and is now a successful broadcaster.
15 F: suddenly dropped … in favour of Alain Prost.
16 E: Often they have to take a pay cut too.

Total = 16 marks

Part 2: A Town Like Davis

17 D: The cars / bicycles contrast is continued in this paragraph.
18 F: Links between 'a group of students' and 'three students'.
19 G: Link between 'energy needs' and 'discourage people from installing air-conditioning'.
20 A: Links between 'houses are restricted …' and 'the size of building plots'.
21 E: Links with 'allotments' in preceding paragraph and 'locally-grown produce' in following paragraph.
22 B: Links between 'personal story' and references to the Hogan family.

Total = 12 marks

Part 3: Whales

23 A: The whale has no voice.
24 C: each sperm whale produces a distinctive series of clicks.
25 D: birdsong is shorter … not so structured as whale song.
26 D: (Obviously whales cannot have really done this.)
27 D: showing where each singer comes from.
28 B: simple songs did not contain any rhyming passages.
29 C: are simply trying to please themselves and their audience.

Total = 14 marks

Part 4: Writers Do It Lying Down

30 F: I get on with writing wherever I am.
31 C/E: my typist Monica.
32 E/C: I found a wonderful lady who can read my writing.
33 B: It's where the word processor lives.
34 A: My study has to be at least 70 degrees.
35 D: I work on a big black electric typewriter.
36 E/F: I used to type the manuscript myself.
37 F/E: I bought a portable typewriter …'Never again'.
38 E: and done the school run.
39 D: I don't very much want to be there.
40 D/E: and will roam off to get mugs of coffee.
41 E/D: I have little breaks for more coffee.
42 A: I like silence.
43 E: When I was single … it's harder now.
44 B/F: I work in a summerhouse … I shut myself into the loft.
45 F/B: to write in the library … or at the kitchen table.
46 C: There's nothing in the middle … not even any food.
47 A: do exactly 35 minutes of yoga.
48 B/C: I video old films. That's my treat.
49 C/B: I'm only fit to slump in front of the telly.

Total = 20 marks

PAPER 2   Writing

Part 1

Question 1

Style: Informal letter to a friend. Start 'Dear Fiona' and end 'Best wishes' and your first name.

Content: Give advice to Fiona – whatever you think best. Mention what you saw at the party and the advertisement you have seen. Refer to the points in Fiona's letter and draw conclusions from the information you have.

Part 2

Question 2

Style: Formal letter. Use formal language.

Content: Mention the survey (refer to numbers / percentages) and summarise opinions and suggestions. Back up suggestions with reasons. The sports named are only examples – you can mention others. Refer to prices / opening hours. Note that leisure facilities (for example, a cafe, social events) are mentioned in the question, as well as sports.

Question 3

Style: Report layout (see Test 1). Use formal language.

Content: Give examples of both vandalism and theft. Suggest solutions to the problems that you mention.

Question 4

Style: This is a review so put the name of the book and the author at the top. You could add an English translation of the title. Use a headline and sub-headings and fairly informal, persuasive language.

Content: Say what kind of book it is. Mention the main characters and summarise the plot, but not in too much detail. Give reasons for recommending it.

Question 5

Style: Report layout (see Test 1). Use a formal register and style.

Content: Mention just two problems, but in some detail. Suggest solutions to both the problems.

PAPER 3   English in Use

There is 1 mark for each correct answer in Parts 1–6.

Part 1: That Sweet Smell Of Success Is …

1 A: B, C and D sound too aggressive in this context.
2 D: The aim is to find out if they work, as in 'trials' of new drugs.
3 B: 'Chain' is the word that goes with 'shops'.
4 A: This is one example from a large number, so 'include' is the word.
5 C: The meaning is that it makes you think of holidays.
6 C: Only 'lasting' collocates with 'quality'.

7 B: An abstract word is needed, not something that physically exists.

8 D: 'Application' refers to the actual use, not just the idea.

9 A: This is the word that goes with supermarkets.

10 B: The meaning is to link two things together, not make them one.

11 C: 'Defeat the object' is a fixed phrase.

12 D: Only 'express' goes with 'image'.

13 C: The reference is to what they might do in the future.

14 A: The meaning is that they have tried everything else and only this is left.

15 B: The meaning is that it is wrong. 'Unjustifiable' has this sense and is the only word to collocate with 'invasion of privacy'.

Part 2: Volcanoes: Dangers And Benefits

16 *do (auxiliary verb):* This word completes the Present Simple question.

17 *such / these (modifier / determiner):* The areas have already been referred to in the first sentence.

18 *no / little (quantifiers):* This refers back to 'poor people'.

19 *which (relative):* It is after a comma, so it cannot be 'that'.

20 *less / smaller (comparative):* 'Than' indicates that we need a comparative.

21 *is (verb):* This verb has 'What' as its subject.

22 *of (preposition):* This is the preposition after 'full'.

23 *although / though (conjunction):* It is followed by a verb phrase, so it cannot be 'despite'.

24 *back (particle):* This is part of the phrasal verb 'pays back'.

25 *by / through (preposition):* These words tell us how something happens.

26 *just / but (adverb):* Obviously there are many other examples.

27 *is (auxiliary verb):* The past participle suggests a passive construction.

28 *makes (verb):* The subject of this verb is 'the way', so it is singular.

29 *among (preposition):* There are many others, so it is not 'between'.

30 *which / that (relative):* This is a defining clause so both these words are correct.

Part 3: Going It Alone

31 *one. I'd*

32 *choose*

33 *receive*

34 *travel*

35 *frightening*

36 ✓

37 *advice*

38 ✓

39 *loan*

40 *success*

41 *case) so*

42 *for. John*

43 ✓

44 *whether*

45 *hasn't*

46 *it's*

Part 4: In Case Of Fire

47 *loss (verb to noun).*

48 *security (adjective to noun).*

49 *authorised (noun to verb).*

50 *warning (verb to adjective).*

51 *electricity (adjective to noun):* It cannot be 'electrical' because the word refers to the supply of electricity.

52 *disabled (adjective to past participle / negative adjective):* Note that two changes are needed to the base word.

53 *belongings (verb to noun).*

Subscribe Now

54 *subscription (verb to noun).*

55 *payment (verb to noun):* It doesn't need to be plural after 'methods'.

56 *administration (verb to noun).*

57 *reduction (verb to noun).*

58 *saving (verb to noun).*

59 *renewing / renewals (adjective to noun).*

60 *automatically (adjective to adverb):* Note that we need a double 'll'.

61 *reminder (verb to noun).*

Part 5: Historical Cottages Trust Booking Terms

62 *in advance:* three months before.

63 *currency / money:* Payments must be made in sterling.

64 *refund:* forfeit the entire booking fee.

65 *blocked / impassable:* prevents you from reaching the property.

66 *arrive:* must not enter the property.

67 *leave:* must not stay longer than.

68 *follow / come after:* and your successors.

69 *all right / O.K. / permissible:* are permitted.

70 *jump / lie:* must be kept off the furniture.

71 *only:* nobody except the people.

72 *very seriously:* we mind very much indeed.

73 *drive:* easily accessible by car.

74 *your own:* sheets and towels are not provided.

Part 6: A Telephone Pioneer: Henry Hunnings (1843–86)

75 B: This contrasts with 'granular carbon'.

76 H: This gives an example of 'gadgets'.

77 I: This follows on from 'asked'.

78 F: This tells us the purpose of forming the company.

79 G: This tells us the consequence of there being so many companies.

80 C: This contrasts with 'At first it failed'.

PAPER 4 Listening

There is 1 mark for each correct answer in Parts 1–4.

Part 1: Safety In The Home

1 *irons:* A child who pulls at the hanging flex of an iron.
2 *cups of coffee / tea:* Cups of tea … Children pull at them …
3 *saucepans:* handles of saucepans … small children can grab them.
(1–3 in any order)
4 *(internal) glass doors:* internal glass doors … make sure they are fitted with safety glass.
5 *(electricity) sockets:* to fit plastic covers to all electricity sockets.
(4–5 in any order)
6 *cleaning products:* cleaning products … Lock them up.
7 *matches:* be very careful not to leave boxes of matches … where children can get their hands on them.
(6–7 in any order)
8 *doors:* checking if a child is behind the door.
9 *door frames:* don't let little children put their fingers in the door frame.
10 *electrical devices:* plugging in electrical devices by themselves.

Part 2: Conference Arrangements

11 *11.30:* is now on Saturday at 11.30.
12 *Lecture Room B:* but it is in Lecture Room B not Lecture Room D.
13 *308:* Just tell the receptionist the number – three hundred and eight.
14 *closes:* nine-thirty p.m. at the latest because that is when reception closes.
15 *Wine Reception:* It will now start at seven fifteen.
16 *refund:* pick up a refund from reception.
17 *key:* pick up the room key from reception.
18 *social programme:* The receptionist will also give you a copy of the revised social programme.
(16–18 in any order)
19 *279 623623:* You can call me on …
20 *8 o'clock:* I will be leaving the office at eight o'clock.

Part 3: Fitness And Health

21 *age:* the first thing to think about is how old you are.
22 *safe / suitable:* Up to … age … 35, you can take up any sport you like.
23 *overweight:* if you are carrying a few extra kilos … you should definitely avoid such sports as squash …
24 *good as before:* Another danger is when people … (expect) to be of the same standard as they were before.
25 *your own pace / speed:* You can control your own pace.
26 *body / weight:* you are supported by the water … or by the saddle.
27 *slim / slimmer / lose weight:* people often … think … exercise will help them get rid of excess fat.
28 *running:* to run for four hours to burn up one hundred grams of fat.
29 *immediately / straightaway / too soon:* go straight into a cold shower … straight into the sauna.

30 *ill / unwell / not well:* professional sportsmen dying because they have continued their training schedule … when they should have been in bed.

Part 4: Accidents

31 E: in those days nobody wore a helmet … you see a lot of people wearing helmets now.
32 H: the bindings didn't release as easily as they do now.
33 C: not even the referee … I was off the rest of the season.
34 G: he wouldn't get over it … it was just too high for him.
35 B: hundreds of miles from anywhere … even with a life jacket.
36 D: I couldn't believe it.
37 C: I felt like a complete idiot.
38 H: It was deliberate. It wasn't an accident at all.
39 G: You have to accept the occasional accident.
40 E: I had no hope at all.

PAPER 5 Speaking

Part 1

At the moment I'm studying … at … .
It's a full-time / part-time course.
In the future, I intend to … / What I hope to do next is … .
Nowadays, students use computers much more than they used to.
Another change I've noticed is that …

Test 3

PAPER 1 Reading

Part 1: Story Of Your Life

1 B: they can see at a glance that you would be capable of the job.
2 A: it will help provide a structure for the interview.
3 A/F: your most critical selling document.
4 F/A: If you can't sell yourself …
5 F: feel comfortable with what you have written …
6 B: Write your CV in the third person.
7 B/F: you should tailor your CV for each job.
8 F/B: you should customise your CV for each job.
9 F: built around your present job or aimed at a change in your career.
10 B: Examine each word you have used …
11 D: you do not need to include your early education …
12 A: get it wrong and your work experience … could be consigned to the waste bin.
13 F: These four to five skills will match what is on the job specification.

14 D: interests should be left to the end (they) are an important part of your CV.

15 E: Use headings … and bullet points to focus on key information.

16 E: Print it on quality paper.

17 C: The interviewer is more interested in what you are doing now.

Total = 17 marks

Part 2: Sleep Easy

18 G: Link with 'sleep disorder' in the following paragraph.

19 E: Links between 'typical insomniacs' and definition of insomnia in the following paragraph.

20 B: Continues description of insomnia from the preceding paragraph.

21 F: Describes solutions for sleeping disorders which are continued in the next paragraph.

22 A: Continues list of self-help measures.

23 D: Gives more information on REM sleep.

Total = 12 marks

Part 3: Still Sprinting

24 D: Jeffrey Archer is not noticeably down and a considerable distance from out.

25 B: literature is not his first love … The writing has to fit into a political schedule.

26 B: It was vitally important to be physically working.

27 D: It happens mainly between six and eight in the morning …

28 B: he accepts innumerable speaking engagements …

29 B: but there's mutual respect …

30 D: He'll get me to build characters … .

Total = 14 marks

Part 4: Springing Hot From The Bowels Of The Earth

31 B: you are greeted by a horrible stench.

32 C: it has now been incorporated in a range of beauty products.

33 A: lured the richest and most fashionable of 19th century Europe.

34 C: A bath of water is run … and mixed with … Moor.

35 D: like broken tarmac rising to meet the power station beyond.

36 C/D: with plain functional accommodation.

37 D/C: The Blue Lagoon is a motel rather than the spa it has ambitions to become.

38 B: scalding water … can catch out the unwary.

39 D: Swathed in white robes with pointed hoods.

40 C: at the expense of the public health services.

41 B: day trippers who come by hydrofoil.

42 C: After half an hour … to rest for an hour.

43 A: waters from twelve springs … makes the spa unique.

44 A: people … heading as one, to the Hall des Sources.

45 B/D: There is no cure centre or facilities.

46 D/B: the lack of facilities …

47 B: the active volcano … with steam issuing from the fissures in its side.

48 C: a fashionable spa centre in medieval times.

Total = 18 marks

PAPER 2 Writing

Part 1

Question 1

Style: Report format (see Test 1). Use formal language.

Content: Refer to the Principal's note. Summarise information from the questionnaire and comments, using words not just percentages. Make recommendations for changes based on your evidence.

Part 2

Question 2

Style: A leaflet should have a main heading and sub-headings. Use informal language.

Content: Describe the goods you want and name the charity. Give reasons for choosing that charity. Give details of the sale, including the collection / delivery of goods.

Question 3

Style: Informal letter to a friend. Begin 'Dear (first name of friend)' and end 'Best wishes (your name)'.

Content: Express sympathy, then make practical suggestions.

Question 4

Style: Brochure with a heading and sub-headings. Use an informal style.

Content: Include sections on transport, food and drink, and entertainment. The phrase 'such things as' in the question means that you can add other topics of your own.

Question 5

Style: Formal letter. Begin 'Dear Mr / Mrs (name of boss)' and end 'Yours sincerely (your full name)'.

Content: Say what you want to do and give your reasons. Mention benefits to the company.

PAPER 3 English in Use

There is 1 mark for each correct answer in Parts 1–6.

Part 1: Shoplifting

1 A: B is too precise, C/D too general.

2 C: This is a well-known fixed phrase.

3 B: The meaning is that the staff are actually there.

4 A: A clearly refers to machines but is not too precise.

5 B: This is part of a fixed phrase.

6 C: The contrast is with the complex electronic methods.
7 B: The idea is that they can see much more.
8 A: 'Field' collocates with 'of vision'.
9 D: The other words are too precise.
10 C: The idea is whether the cards are genuine or not.
11 A: The electronic systems are faster.
12 D: This is a fixed phrase.
13 B: It is what the thieves are aiming for.
14 A: The fact that they can be carried away makes it easy for thieves to steal them.
15 D: The meaning is that the police might find them.

Part 2: Across The Gap

16 *from (preposition):* linking verb and noun.
17 *such:* part of fixed phrase meaning 'for example'.
18 *deal (noun):* collocates with 'great'.
19 *able (verb):* follows 'to be'.
20 *some / certain (determiner):* preceding noun.
21 *but (conjunction):* expressing a contrast.
22 *will / can (modal verb):* followed by main verb.
23 *when / if (conjunction):* referring to time / condition.
24 *without (preposition):* followed by gerund.
25 *which (relative):* preceding main verb.
26 *like (preposition):* giving an example / comparison.
27 *to:* part of the infinitive 'to support'.
28 *another (determiner):* followed by a noun.
29 *because / as / since (conjunction):* giving a reason.
30 *at / for (preposition):* followed by gerund.

Part 3: Are Women More Romantic Than Men?

31 *just*
32 *they*
33 *of*
34 *it*
35 ✓
36 *how*
37 *organised*
38 *be*
39 ✓
40 *the*
41 *regard*
42 *themselves*
43 ✓
44 *so*
45 *the*
46 ✓

Part 4: A New Restaurant

47 *restoration (verb to noun).*
48 *unknown (verb to adjective).*
49 *archaeologists (abstract noun to concrete noun).*
50 *discoveries (verb to noun).*
51 *integration (verb to noun).*
52 *romantic (noun to adjective).*
53 *attraction (verb to noun).*

A New Way To Get To The Airport

54 *opening (adjective to noun).*
55 *operation (verb to noun).*
56 *economical (noun to adjective).*
57 *spacious (noun to adjective).*
58 *attendants (verb to noun).*
59 *flights (verb to noun).*
60 *preference (verb to noun).*
61 *unpleasant (verb to noun).*

Part 5: Staff In-Service Training Scheme

62 *fortnight:* 14-day.
63 *previous experience:* Suitable for complete beginners.
64 *except:* you must bring your own boots.
65 *a few:* Places are very limited.
66 *the end:* before January 31st.
67 *been before / been already / tried it / done it:* who attended this course in March.
68 *last:* … in March.
69 *go again:* cannot re-apply.
70 *free:* There is no charge.
71 *advantage:* will improve the chances.
72 *good enough:* reach an adequate standard.
73 *how well / about what:* a full report … during the course.
74 *losing / giving up:* taken as part of your annual leave.

Part 6: Why You Feel Under The Weather

75 E: Links with 'growing numbers'.
76 G: Links with 'tropics'.
77 H: Contrast between 'temperate' and 'tropic'.
78 F: Links between 'sufferers' and 'they'.
79 C: Links between 'low temperatures' and 'winter'.
80 A: Links between strong adverbs – amazingly, acutely, completely.

PAPER 4   Listening

Part 1: Electric Cars

There is 1 mark for each correct answer in Parts 1–4.

1 *nineteenth century:* as long ago as 1899.
2 *faster / very fast:* no petrol-driven car could manage anything like that speed.
3 *two alternatives / approaches / speed or distance:* a very short distance at high speed or … a longer distance at a modest speed.
4 *very far:* The former was what Jenatzy went for.
5 *pollute / cause pollution:* there are no exhaust fumes.
6 *sources of power / motors / engines:* an electric unit and a tiny petrol engine.
7 *sun / solar panels:* solar panels on the roof.
8 *at home:* plug it into the mains at night.
9 *purely / only electric:* two motors … both electric.
10 *(very) well:* good performance even for a petrol-driven car.

Part 2: A Dissatisfied Customer

11 *Dr / Doctor*: My name is Dr John Smith.
12 *37 King Street*: I live at 37 King Street.
13 *445 446 2993*.
14 *FM 2500*.
15 *13 January*: the invoice … was on 13 January.
16 *1SM114*: customer code 1SM114.
17 *not received*: the adaptor was not inside.
18 *Martin Brown*: the salesperson was called … Martin Brown.
19 *adaptor*.
20 *two days*: can't wait any longer than two more days.

Part 3: The Uses Of Graphology

21 *'You and Your Handwriting'*: author of …
22 *selection procedures*: who has made a particular study of selection procedures.
23 *ambition*: deep psychological traits, ambition.
24 *sensitivity to others*: sensitivity to other people.
25 *broad-mindedness*: how broad-minded you are.
(23–25 in any order)
26 *the expense*: a consultation is quite expensive.
27 *executive posts*: high-level appointments.
28 *one-to-one interviews*: the interview, a one-to one situation.
29 *(very) weak / unreliable / unconvincing*: this technique doesn't come up with what it's meant to.
30 *losing their jobs*: afraid they'll take over their jobs.

Part 4: The Prizewinners

31 A: a speech from 'Romeo and Juliet'.
32 C: the next day the principal … called me in.
33 B: the chance of a portrait commission.
34 C: it's only now really that I'm beginning to do what I really want.
35 B: my flute-playing really seemed to appeal to them.
36 A: I kept to my original plan.
37 C: as part of the prize I had the chance to give two performances in New York.
38 B: a contract with a leading classical company.
39 B: and then I realised I was actually good at academic subjects.
40 A: I was too successful too young. Life's better now …

PAPER 5

Part 1

At the moment I'm living in …
I like it quite a lot because …
In comparison with …
It's much better than … because.
I hope I will have the opportunity to live in …
Ideally, I would like to live in …
For me, the perfect place to live would be …

Test 4

PAPER 1   Reading

Part 1: Writing On The Wall

1 D: she works part-time for another large literary agent.
2 E: he snapped up the twenty-one year old.
3 B: I thought publishers would look down on us as amateurs.
4 A: The first acknowledgement … were her tutors.
5 C: something often missing from courses elsewhere … declining to point the finger.
6 E: He has his eye on another three or four writers but refuses to elaborate.
7 C: the last thing publishers … look forward to is a huge slush-pile slithering through their door.
8 F: where by chance he met Clare Wigfall.
9 B: I was suspicious of creative writing programmes.
10 D: Although intimidating … for Anna Davis.
11 B: you may not be able to teach people to write.
12 D: On a course, you've got a captive audience to give you proper attention.
13 F: After reading two of her short stories.
14 B: spent a large part of my career as an academic who wrote novels.
15 C: the course gives them a degree of scepticism and realistic expectation.
16 D: Her superb first novel … is to be published in January.

Total = 16 marks

Part 2: Terrorised By A Collar Stud

17 C: This paragraph has examples of the 'little phrases'.
18 F: 'the haberdashery shop' links with 'this shop'.
19 G: 'He was very nice' links with 'the man in the furniture shop'.
20 A: Links with 'my brother'.
21 D: Links with '11 plus'.
22 B: 'She got us all to lie down' links with 'speech therapist'.

Total = 12 marks

Part 3: Desert Discoveries And Monster Myths

23 A: all the babies are of the same colony.
24 C: many … may not be separate species after all.
25 B: neither round nor oval but long and thin.
26 B: dug the nest with her hind legs.
27 B: ten per cent longer than any Old World dinosaur found so far.
28 B: mammal-style binocular vision.

Total = 12 marks

Part 4: Best Of Times Worst Of Times

29 B: my excitement comes from working … a nightmare.
30 E: I had to pick her up.

31	A:	There are no towns or shops … It was perfect.
32	B:	My wife and son were not upset because they know my nature.
33	C/D:	I was sent back several years running.
34	D/C:	we went year after year.
35	F:	I'd forgotten to have the jabs.
36	D:	I pretended I loved the seaside.
37	A:	go for invigorating walks.
38	C:	I hated tennis … and was afraid of horses.
39	D:	We went on jolly outings when it wasn't raining.
40	E:	It probably wasn't the best time to learn … April.
41	F:	There was a bullring in Marseilles … I was terrified.
42	B/C/D:	I was pressurised into going.
43	B/C/D:	I was sent to boarding school.
44	B/C/D:	where we went year after year, and it was absolute hell.
45	D:	My father hated everything.
46	E:	I reached a farm and was attacked by three dogs.

Total = 18 marks

PAPER 2 Writing

Part 1

Question 1

Style: Informal leaflet.

Content: The essential part of the leaflet is a revised timetable incorporating the new information. There are several possibilities. The rest of the leaflet should add detail by describing the refreshments, prize-giving and social events. The leaflet should have a heading and sub-headings. It should emphasise the attractions of the event.

Part 2

Question 2

Style: Informal and fairly light.

Content: A headline is needed. The sub-headings could be 'My greatest fear', etc. Note the words 'some or all' mean that it is not necessary to include everything.

Question 3

Style: Informal letter to a friend.

Content: Express sympathy. Comment on the three problems mentioned and reassure your friend by expressing optimism.

Question 4

Style: Formal letter. Begin 'Dear Sir or Madam' and end 'Yours faithfully'.

Content: Refer to the competition. State your chosen prize and give reasons for your choice.

Question 5

Style: Report (see Test 1). Use formal language.

Content: Name the hotel and describe the location. Comment on the room, facilities and the service. Make your recommendation (or not – your report may be positive or negative).

PAPER 3 English in Use

There is 1 mark for each correct answer in Parts 1–6.

Part 1: You Must Remember This

1	A
2	B
3	C
4	D
5	B
6	C
7	A
8	D
9	A
10	A
11	D
12	A
13	A
14	B
15	D

Part 2: The Development Of The Modern Motor Car

16	*had / reached / achieved*
17	*for*
18	*of*
19	*a*
20	*It*
21	*enough*
22	*may / might*
23	*this / the*
24	*it*
25	*much*
26	*could*
27	*This*
28	*its / the / his*
29	*their*
30	*them*

Part 3: Why Do People Fail To Help When They Should?

31	*being's*
32	*Fortunately*
33	*normal people*
34	*another, fail*
35	✓
36	✓
37	✓
38	*centuries*
39	*answers. One*
40	*someone, or*
41	*seldom*
42	*However, we*
43	*different*
44	✓
45	*emergency*
46	✓

Part 4: Terrified Customers

47 *nervous (noun to adjective).*
48 *difficulty (adjective to noun).*
49 *slippery (verb to adjective).*
50 *enthusiast (verb to noun).*
51 *enquiries (verb to noun).*
52 *unfriendly (noun to adjective).*
53 *poisonous (noun to adjective).*

Personal Presentation

54 *employment (verb to noun).*
55 *consultation (verb to noun).*
56 *impression (verb to noun).*
57 *jewellery / jewelry (noun to noun).*
58 *excessively (noun to adverb).*
59 *inappropriate (adjective to negative adjective).*
60 *acceptable (verb to adjective).*
61 *length (adjective to noun).*

Part 5: Superdog Shot In Mouth

62 *wealthy / rich / affluent*
63 *Each of*
64 *waved about*
65 *the manager*
66 *hand over*
67 *shaking / trembling*
68 *floor*
69 *bit*
70 *teeth*
71 *confused*
72 *taking anything / any money / the money / the cash*
73 *immediately / quickly*
74 *will recover*

Part 6: Aspects Of Love

75 F
76 E
77 G
78 D
79 C
80 B

There is 1 mark for each correct answer in Parts 1–4.

Part 1: An Accident At The Roundabout

1 *on the balcony of*
2 *sports car*
3 *white*
4 *(Post Office) van*
5 *red*
6 *twice*

7 *large, dirty*
8 *old, slow*
9 *three*
10 *injured / hurt / hit*

Part 2: The Red Planet

11 *6,786*
12 *38 %*
13 *43 %*
14 *687*
15 *24 hours 37 minutes*
16 *2*
17 *small / smaller*
18 *Carbon dioxide*
19 *0.1 %*
20 *24,000*

Part 3: Electronic Books

21 M
22 MR
23 R
24 M
25 R
26 R
27 MR
28 MR
29 MR
30 M

Part 4: Danger And Risk

31 D
32 G
33 C
34 H
35 B
36 H
37 D
38 B
39 F
40 C

Part 1

My favourite kind of holiday is …
The best holiday I ever had was in …
I would like to try …
I prefer to … rather than …

Test 5

Part 1: The Power Of The Spoken Word

1   B: Practised orators … were critical in helping to form opinions.

2   B: a work called *Rhetorica* … to argue successfully.

3   A: Until the beginning of this century … a proper education.

4   C: Whether he would be impressed by what he heard … is another matter.

5   D: Firstly, you should decide what you think.

6   F: You should also anticipate your opponent's arguments … winning over your audience.

7   G: You might want to deal with … convincing arguments first … On the other hand.

8   G/E: You also need to present it properly.

9   E/G: It often helps to think of specific examples.

10   D: An opinion which has … you need to understand what you are talking about.

11   B: Shakespeare, who knew … Roman art of public speaking.

12   A: If you say … But this need not necessarily be so.

13   A: It is far more likely to get you out of trouble than into it.

14   D: The same basic principles underlie most systems.

15   D: It is surprising … without really deciding what they think.

16   B: In these ancient societies, writing was used less widely.

17   C: Whether he would be impressed … is another matter.

Total = 17 marks

Part 2: Simply The Best

18   B: Describes the result of the competition mentioned in paragraph 1.

19   A: Links between 'major project', 'my first task' and 'the deep end'.

20   D: Links between 'mixing with staff' and 'in touch with staff throughout the company'.

21   E: Arguments against the idea that 'the secretarial role is often undervalued'.

22   G: Links between Total Quality Management and 'management structure and theories'.

23   C: Links between 'ignorance of the real world' and 'I could write essays … but I knew nothing about business'.

Total = 12 marks

Part 3: Fast Forward

24   C: a growing divide between those with too much work and those without any.

25   C: These pressures aren't confined to executives and professionals.

26   A: time remains off the political agenda.

27   D: we could … see every seventh year taken off as a matter of course.

28   C: it sets goals and stretches capacities.

29   B: but rather to achieve more autonomy.

Total = 12 marks

Part 4: They Said I Was Useless But Look At Me Now

30   A: I felt guilty because my parents had spent so much money.

31   C: I always wanted to be a journalist but.

32   B: Working-class people like us don't do things like that.

33   A: For the first time in my life I felt really charged up.

34   C: But the college still kicked me out.

35   D: The atmosphere at the poly was so laid back.

36   B: sent off the manuscript to an agent … managed to sell it for £150,000.

37   B: I loved primary school … really boring.

38   A: I can honestly say my education is irrelevant.

39   A/C: I went on to further education college … I failed the lot.

40   C/A: at art college … I discovered that I couldn't draw.

41   A: I started getting frustrated … had no budgetary responsibility.

42   D: At secondary school I was having to run to catch up.

43   C: I don't care whether they've been to university.

44   D: an MA in silversmithing … they passed me.

45   A/B: I think the ability to sell is innate.

46   B/A: I sometimes think that writing talent is innate.

47   C: I started a graphics course … against the wishes of my father.

48   B: I left school at 15, which was illegal.

49   C: the sculpture teacher … the best advice anyone ever gave me.

Total = 20 marks

Part 1

Question 1

Style: Letter a is formal in style. Letter b is informal.

Content: The letter to the hotel must be persuasive and make out a good case. In the letter to Tom and Sarah, you may decide to return their money or not – you could impose conditions.

Part 2

Question 2

Style: Informal, but with suitable headings to summarise the points you are making.

Content: Give your opinion on the exhibits and how they are displayed, the information about them which is available, the refreshments and souvenirs. Add some more categories of your own. Your comments can be positive or negative or a mixture of both.

Question 3

Style: Informal letter to a friend.

Content: Give advice to your friend about the advantages of remaining in your own country and the disadvantages of living abroad.

Question 4

Style: Magazine article. Use a headline and sub-headings. Use an informal style.

Content: Say something about the lessons, the teachers, the buildings and the social programme. Add extra topics of your own. You should be generally positive.

Question 5

Style: You are writing a magazine article about a job, so use fairly formal language. Use a headline and sub-headings.

Content: Describe the place where you work, the range of work that you do, your future prospects, your salary and holidays. Be positive.

PAPER 3 English in Use

There is 1 mark for each correct answer in Parts 1–6.

Part 1: Food For Astronauts

1   C
2   D
3   D
4   B
5   C
6   D
7   A
8   C
9   A
10   C
11   C
12   A
13   B
14   D
15   D

Part 2: Chess

16   *have*
17   *than*
18   *were*
19   *as*
20   *which / who*
21   *it*
22   *had*
23   *most*
24   *Until / Before*
25   *but*
26   *in*
27   *it*
28   *without*
29   *else*
30   *all*

Part 3: Marriage

31   *themselves*
32   *they*
33   ✓
34   ✓
35   *possibly*
36   *for*
37   *it*
38   *been*
39   *by*
40   ✓
41   *are*
42   *a*
43   *has*
44   *least*
45   *such*
46   ✓

Part 4: An Opportunity to Save Money on Books

47   *depth (adjective to noun).*
48   *outstanding (verb to adjective).*
49   *indispensable (verb to adjective).*
50   *publication (verb to noun).*
51   *instalments (verb to noun).*
52   *ensures (adjective to verb).*
53   *investment (verb to noun).*

Changes In The High Street

54   *arrangements (verb to noun).*
55   *complaints (verb to noun).*
56   *residents (verb to noun).*
57   *intention (verb to noun).*
58   *unfortunately (noun to adverb).*
59   *collisions (verb to noun).*
60   *annoyance (verb to noun).*
61   *improvements (verb to noun).*

Part 5: For Sale

62   *goes back / dates back / belongs*
63   *about half*
64   *dates from*
65   *no need*
66   *excellent condition*
67   *nearly / almost / about*
68   *the possibility / the opportunity*
69   *plenty of / enough*
70   *land*
71   *facilities*
72   *keep fit / exercise*
73   *well-protected / protected*
74   *negotiation*

Part 6: The Pull Of The Land

75   B
76   G
77   I

78 C
79 E
80 A

PAPER 4   Listening

There is 1 mark for each correct answer in Parts 1–4.

Part 1: The History Of The Telephone

1 *£45*
2 *a year's wages*
3 *in country houses*
4 *manual exchanges*
5 *reduction in cost*
6 *increase in numbers*
(4–6 in any order)
7 *through the operator*
8 *1970s / 1975*
9 *slow / unreliable*
10 *unreliable / slow*

Part 2: Weekend Attractions

11 *engine sheds / old steam trains*
12 *telegraph office*
13 *post office*
(11–13 in any order)
14 *Fairbourne (born / e)*
15 *ferry*
16 *Italy*
17 *10.45*
18 *horse-drawn / electric*
19 *electric / horse-drawn*
20 *teddy (bear)*

Part 3

21 C
22 B
23 A
24 C
25 B
26 C
27 C
28 C

Part 4: Performing In Public

29 H
30 B
31 C
32 G
33 F
34 F
35 D
36 E
37 A
38 B

PAPER 5   Speaking

Part 1

I think I would rather ... than ...
I enjoy being by myself
I'd rather spend my spare time mixing with other people.
A few years ago I used to ... but now I ...
Compared with a few years ago, I find that now I tend to ...

Tapescripts

Test 1

PART 1   Course Information

You will hear a lecturer talking to students at the beginning of their course. For questions 1–10, fill in the missing information. You will hear the recording twice.

Well, good morning everyone. My first task this morning, and it's a very happy one for me to perform, is to welcome all of you to this first tutorial for the University of Brancaster course A753 on Art in Italy. I'll be passing around a paper on which I'd like you to write your names, so that I know exactly who's been present, and, as is the case for all tutorials, this also means that if anyone who should be here is not, then I'll be able to put any of the handouts given out during the tutorial in the post, so that you'll get the essential information in some form or other, if not necessarily from the horse's mouth. Now there are two basic areas that I intend to deal with today. Past experience has shown that students starting the course have two areas of anxiety: the first is with how their work is going to be assessed, and the second is how best to study for the course.

As you will know if you've read the information sent to course participants before the start of the course, you will be required to supply four pieces of written work for assessment purposes. Each of these Tutor Marked Assignments or TMA's as we call them must be submitted by the date laid down in your course details, and it's absolutely necessary to meet this requirement. No late assignments will be marked, whatever the reason, whatever the reason for their being late, and your grade for the course will be affected.

Now I have some more important remarks to make about the actual mechanics of TMA writing. Although, as I have said, it is essential that you submit your assignment by the required date, I don't want you to feel too worried when you sit down to write the first one. Regard it as a chance to learn from the mistakes you're bound to make.

Word length is always laid down, and for the first TMA it is 2,000 words. You can regard this as a guide, and anything within 500 words either way will be acceptable. Remember that it is important to consider the question carefully and address yourself to the relevant issues. Length isn't an automatic indicator of quality. Legibility is

important, it always helps if what you've written is easy to read. For this reason, we always prefer assignments to be typed if at all possible. If this is not possible, then please write as clearly as you can, allowing good margins so that comments can be written in. And it will help if you write on one side of the paper only. You'll also be receiving a separately written report on what you've submitted, with a grade.

At the end of your assignment, be sure to include all your sources of information – a bibliography including information about the publisher and date should appear at the end of the assignment, and don't forget to acknowledge quotations. Now before I move on to talk about how best to study for the course, would anyone like to ask any questions?

PART 2   Travel News

You will hear a radio announcement about travel problems on the railway. For questions 11–20, complete the notes according to the information you hear, using one or two words a time. Listen very carefully as you will hear the recording once only.

We now have more news about the derailment which happened earlier this morning on the main railway line from Wales to London Paddington. This is causing a lot of problems for passengers travelling into London from the West. It appears that just before 7 a.m. this morning, to be precise at 6.55 a.m., a goods train came off the track just to the west of Swindon. This has blocked the main line from Wales to London. Luckily, the latest reports from police and ambulance crews who have reached the scene indicate that no one has been killed or injured. There were no passengers on the train itself, and the driver is uninjured although in a state of shock. However, the derailment has blocked the track completely and it will be some hours before the line can be cleared. The accident was not caused by concrete blocks on the line, as earlier reported, but by a fallen tree which was blown down in last night's storm.

This accident means that all trains from cities in South Wales, that is from Swansea, Cardiff and Newport, will be subject to heavy delay and many services will be cancelled. These trains, and I repeat, it is trains from

Swansea, Cardiff and Newport, will take an alternative route through Bristol and Bath. Because of this, they will arrive at London Paddington approximately one hour later than the time given in the timetable.

According to the latest information, trains that start their journey in Wales will be affected. Trains from the West of England which pass through Swindon are not affected. Those from Gloucester to Swindon are not affected either. Passengers travelling from Bristol, Bath and Chippenham to London Paddington should therefore experience no delays. These services are operating normally. However, trains travelling from Paddington to these West of England destinations are likely to suffer some delays. We understand that trains to Wales from London Paddington will take an alternative, and much longer route via Gloucester, instead of via Swindon. This will result in considerably increased journey times due to many more trains than usual on this route. You probably need to allow at least an extra hour and a half to reach your destination and if your journey isn't absolutely necessary, it might be best to travel on another day.

So it's not a very good day for travellers from Wales into London, and a very poor day indeed for anyone wanting to travel out of London Paddington to the West. However, the rest of the rail network is operating normally.

PART 3   Actresses At Work

You will hear a radio interview with a researcher, Shirley Grainger, who has been investigating the working situation of actresses. For questions 21–30, complete the statements. You will hear the recording twice.

Interviewer: The results of a comprehensive statistical survey confirm what actresses have known for a long time – that there are fewer roles for women and that when actresses do work, they're less well paid than men and play younger roles. I spoke to Shirley Grainger who was asked by the Actors' Union to investigate the situation. What did her survey reveal?

Shirley Grainger: The union was very concerned about the anecdotal evidence they were getting when women were complaining that they were getting a raw deal and were not getting a proper chance to practise their art. But without hard evidence, which comes from a scientific investigation of the problem, it's very difficult to persuade the producers that there is a problem that they ought to be addressing. So, I had the task of getting the data together. To do this, I interviewed people from different branches of the profession, and was able to gather 35,000 pieces of information which I could then analyse.

Interviewer: So what kind of information was this?

Shirley Grainger: I got information about gender, age, types of role played and earnings, and I looked at people in the theatre, on TV and radio over a three year period. And the figures were really striking – I found differences between actors and actresses in all the fields surveyed, and these differences were significant at a very high level. In TV for instance, men were twice as likely to be employed as women, but in radio that ratio went down even further, with women having only a one in three chance of getting an acting part when compared with men.

Interviewer: Wow . . .

Shirley Grainger: Yes . . . the other key finding was that women in the acting profession have their busiest working life in their twenties and thirties, whereas for men, the busiest time is when they're in their forties. And in fact, by the time they are forty, women drop out of radio and TV altogether.

Interviewer: Well, these really are startling findings, aren't they? I mean, they do confirm what lots of people have been saying, but it's quite something to get this information in black and white.

Shirley Grainger: Yes, and of course, that was precisely the role of the survey to provide firm evidence. Another important thing is pay. The rates of pay in radio, for example, are based on experience, so as long as there are fewer parts for women, this creates a vicious circle. There are far fewer parts for women, so they have less chance to gain experience. Then, when a women does manage to get a part, she's paid less to do it.

Interviewer: So what do producers feel about this situation?

Shirley Grainger: They have tended to argue that in terms of pay, once women get the work, there is equality of treatment and they get paid the same, but our findings prove that this is not the case. In 95 per cent of the cases, women came off worse than men. This new information means that the union will now be able to argue a much stronger case.

Interviewer: But women can only work if the parts are written for them …

Shirley Grainger: Of course, and here there's a bit of passing the buck. The producers say they are just choosing materials that reflects the world and the way it is. They make the point, and I don't know how valid this is, that dramatic situations are more likely to be found in the world of work, particularly in dangerous professions, where they argue men are still in the majority. Then they blame the writers, who they say don't write enough parts for women, especially plum parts. The poor writers say they don't have any power anyway, and so they can't be expected to initiate change. On radio, the audience figures show there's a 55 to 45 per cent ratio of women to men listening in the afternoon when a lot of drama goes out, so there's a pretty clear case for providing drama that caters to this particular group. But it doesn't mean that these dramas necessarily need to have a domestic context.

Interviewer: So in practical terms how do you hope the union is going to use your findings?

Shirley Grainger: Well, it seems that one simple thing that producers can be encouraged to do is to monitor the use of actors and actresses, and then look at these figures in comparison with the sort of figures they would like to be seeing. A more equitable profession is something many actresses would welcome. Also in new plays, where the cast list indicates a profession – be it a nurse, detective, judge and so on, producers could consider what gender this role should be. There's no reason for rigid stereotyping these days. Without this sort of monitoring it's difficult to see how any change is likely to come about. The union will have to be consistent in its pressure for there to be an effect.

PART 4 Losing Your Job

You will hear five short extracts in which different people talk about losing jobs.
Task one: for questions 31–35, match the extracts as you hear them with the professions, listed A–H.
Task two: for questions 36–40, match the extracts as you hear them with the statements about the speakers, listed A–H.
Remember that you must complete both tasks as you listen. You will hear the recording twice.

1

I was called into the office our new Managing Director and told that I was no longer required. I had no reason to suppose that my work had any cause for dissatisfaction – I mean my typing was always up to scratch and I knew from my friends that I was a popular person in the office. But the company had introduced lots of new equipment – word-processors, personal computers and so on so the executives didn't need so much back-up – they could prepare and print their own reports. I felt as if I'd completely lost control of my work situation. Like lots of people, I'm buying my house on a mortgage and I've had to reschedule repayments to the bank now that there's no money coming in. I'm just hoping I'll find something soon.

2

One of the things to recognise in this situation is that you are going to feel a bit up and down – and that's quite normal – but there's a lot you can do to minimise the transition from having a job to not having one. The first thing to do is to get yourself organised, you know, set up a room in your house as a sort of headquarters or office, make sure your filing system is right, all this will give you a boost. Make sure you structure your day, and start off by getting up at the usual time and taking care with your appearance. That's one of the first things that people let go, and it's a big mistake.

3

Everyone in the agency was aware there'd been problems going on and over the months there'd been a reduction in the number of accounts I was responsible for. I mean, with the recession and everything, companies just didn't seem to want to spend so much on promoting their products. Anyway, the director called us in and said that the company was finished, it had gone bust, and we'd all have to go that very day. And we thought, well, this won't be too bad, we'll get some redundancy money, but he said, no, there wouldn't be any and we'd just have to try to get some money from government funds. It still hasn't sunk in yet. I don't know how I'm going to manage.

4

Of course like other firms, I find my company just doesn't have so many vacancies to fill in the present economic climate but yes, we do try to be fair when we've got jobs to offer, and we don't look unfavourably on applicants just because they've been out of work for more than a year. If they've got the qualifications we're looking for and can put together a persuasive curriculum vitae, we'll give them the benefit of the doubt and get them to come along for an interview. We're always on the lookout for people who've seen redundancy as a positive step, something that gives them a kick-start for new opportunities.

5

I landed this big part in a long-running serial which went out three times a week and I was in front of the cameras for nine consecutive months – pretty good experience for a novice like me – but the end came pretty swiftly. The show was going down in the ratings and the powers that be decided we were for the chop and the show came off within a month. After that I spent six months 'resting' before anything at all came up. Quite a change of lifestyle I can tell you, with no money coming in at all.

Test 2

PART 1 Safety In The Home

You will hear a short talk about safety in the home. For questions 1–10, fill in the missing information. You will hear the recording twice.

Presenter: Hello and welcome to the second programme in our series on 'Safety in the Home'. Today Amanda Brown talks about how to protect small children from danger.

Amanda Brown: Hello! Well, this may seem a really obvious point but you should always remember that small children are, well, small and therefore see things from a completely different angle. They are often looking up at things that we grown-ups are looking down on. This means that children often can't see what is on a table. Let me give you an example. A child who pulls at the hanging flex of an iron which is on a table probably can't see the iron, only the brightly-coloured flex. So be careful about the use of irons. They are hot as well as heavy. Cups of tea and coffee left on the table can also be a problem. Children pull at them and get splashed and often burned. For the same reason, always turn the handles of saucepans inwards when they are on the cooker. Don't leave them sticking out because small children can grab them and cause hot liquid to fall down on them, which can have really serious consequences indeed.

As well as pulling at things, children like to run about a lot, so if you have any internal glass doors in your house make sure they are fitted with safety glass. If they are not, and you can't afford to replace them, you can cover them with plastic film. Also, don't have bottles of cleaning products on the floor where children can easily find them. Lock them up or keep them out of reach.

Another big danger is doors opening and closing. You should always open doors slowly and carefully, checking if a child is behind the door. And don't let little children put their fingers in the door frame. This is really dangerous and can cause serious injuries. If you see children doing this, warn them not to.

Because little children like to put their fingers in dangerous places, it is advisable to fit plastic covers to all electricity sockets. This stops small fingers from going in and it also prevents small children from plugging in electrical devices by themselves and possibly causing fires or injuring themselves in some way. Whenever you use the socket, remember to put the cover back on.

And finally, and I think most importantly of all, be very careful not to leave boxes of matches in places where children can get their hands on them. This is very dangerous indeed and can have disastrous consequences.

PART 2 Conference Arrangements

You will hear a message on your answerphone about important changes to the timetable of a conference that you are going to. For questions 11–20, complete the notes according to the information you hear. Listen very carefully as you will hear the recording once only.

Hello, this is Elizabeth Jenkins, conference secretary. I'm ringing you at home because we have had to make some last minute changes to the conference arrangements and these affect you. There isn't time to write to you before the start of the conference, which, as you know, is this coming Friday. For reasons that I won't got into now, because they're a bit complicated, we have had to shorten the conference by half a day – it will now finish at lunchtime on Sunday – and this has had a knock-on effect on various activities. As far as you are concerned, it means that the talk that you are going to give is now on Saturday at 11.30 a.m. and not at 2.30 p.m. as we told you previously. It is still timed to last for one hour so you will finish just in time for lunch, which begins at 12.30.

We hope this does not cause you too much inconvenience and we apologise for having to make this change. The place of your talk is still the same – the Science Block – but it is in Lecture Room B not Lecture Room D, and you will need to ask the porter to open it for you as it is normally kept locked. We have made this change because Room B has the video equipment that you requested and Room D doesn't.

The room in which you will be staying has also been changed, I'm afraid. It is now room 308 in the Rochester Building. You can pick up the room key from reception when you arrive. Just tell the receptionist the number – 308 – and she'll give you the key. Please remember that you have to arrive before 9.30 p.m. at the latest because that is when the reception closes.

The time of the Wine Reception has also been changed. It will now start at 7.15 and last for about an hour, finishing just before dinner at 8.15. When you arrive remember to pick up a refund from reception. We have to make a small refund because the conference is half a day shorter than planned. Since it is quite small we will pay it to you in cash at the conference. The receptionist will also give you a copy of the revised social programme, although fortunately the changes to the social programme have been very small.

If any of this isn't completely clear, please feel free to ring me back. You can call me on 279 623623. I will be leaving the office at eight o'clock tonight but I'll be back at nine tomorrow morning.

You will hear a radio interview with a doctor, about health and sport. For questions 21–30, complete each of the statements. You will hear the recording twice.

Interviewer: Hello and welcome to 'Questions and Answers'. Dr David Green, who is a specialist in sports medicine, has joined us in the studio today and has some good advice for people who are thinking of taking up a sport. Dr Green, what factors do you think we should consider if we are thinking of taking up a sport?

Dr Green: Well, the first thing to think about is how old you are. Up to about the age of, say, thirty-five, you can take up any sport you like, providing that you have no particular medical problems. If you are carrying a few extra kilos, or if you smoke, you should definitely avoid such sports as squash, fencing and judo. By the age of sixty five, even healthy people should avoid those sports.

Interviewer: Really? Why do you say that?

Dr Green: Because such sports involve sudden bursts of energy which are not completely under your control. You have to respond to what your opponent is doing or to what the ball is doing. There can be sudden and rapid increases in the heartbeat, and this can cause problems for some people. In addition, the sudden and unpredictable movements can cause people to fall over and injure themselves that way.

Interviewer: But some people may have been practising these sports all their lives. Should they give up when they reach a certain age?

Dr Green: No, no, that's a different matter. If people have been practising sports regularly all their lives they can probably continue for as long as they feel like it. What we are talking about is taking up sports for the first time. You sometimes read in the newspapers about elderly people taking up karate, for example. This really isn't a good idea. Another danger is when people who practised a sport when they were young, don't do it for a few years, and then take it up again expecting to be the same standard as they were before. They often attempt too much and suffer injuries. In fact, such people should start again from the beginning and build up gradually to their previous standard.

Interviewer: Are there any sports or physical activities which are generally safe and suitable for everyone, even people who are older and perhaps not in the best of health?

Dr Green: Well, probably the safest of all is walking, fairly vigorous and energetic walking, that is, which is safe for everyone. But sports such as swimming or cycling are a good choice because you can control your own pace and go as slowly or as fast as you wish. That is the big difference, compared with those sports we mentioned earlier. Another plus point is that you are supported by the water if you are swimming, or by the saddle if you are on a bike. This means that you don't get the problems caused by repeated impact of the foot on the ground, which you do get with running. But even when people have chosen the right sport for their age and fitness level, they often go about things in the wrong way.

Interviewer: Do they? Can you give some examples of that?

Dr Green: Well, people often want to get a bit slimmer and they think that doing more exercise will help them get rid of excess fat, but it won't, at least not by itself. You have to combine exercise with a calorie-controlled diet – then you will get results. What people often don't realise is that it takes hours and hours of exercise to burn up tiny amounts of fat. You would have to run for four hours to burn up one hundred grams of fat, for example. And if people have exercised a lot they feel pleased with themselves and decide that they deserve an ice-cream, or something like that, and just put back on the calories they have lost.

Interviewer: Even if people have that wrong idea, they probably won't come to any harm, though. Are there things people do which can lead to serious problems?

Dr Green: Well, yes. Another misconception is to do with cooling down after exercise. Most people understand the vital importance of warming up before you start exercising. If you don't do that you risk tearing muscles and ligaments. However, when they finish exercising, many people go straight into a cold shower, or even worse, straight into the sauna. These are really very bad things to do. It is vital to cool down because sudden changes of temperature are not good for you, in fact, they can be very dangerous. If you go straight into a sauna, for example, your already high temperature will go even higher and your heart may begin to beat very fast.

Interviewer: Well, I have certainly seen many people do just that. I suppose that professional sportsmen don't make such mistakes.

Dr Green: Well, I'm not so sure about that. There is one thing that professional sportsmen do, because of the intense competitive pressure that they are under, which is one of the most dangerous things that anyone can do. It is to continue to exercise when they have a cold or minor infection. There have been more than a few cases of professional sportsmen dying because they have continued with their training schedule when they should have been in bed. So if you are feeling under the weather, stop your exercise programme until you have fully recovered.

PART 4   Accidents

You will hear five short extracts in which different people talk about accidents that they have had. Task one: for questions 31–35, match the extracts as you hear them with the types of accident, listed A–H.
Task two: for questions 36–40, match the extracts as you hear them with the different feelings experienced immediately after the accident by the speakers, listed A–H.
Remember that you must complete both tasks as you listen. You will hear the recording twice.

1

Well, I couldn't believe it. I just looked up and there it was right in front of me. I mean, it shouldn't have been there. It'd just pulled out suddenly. I couldn't avoid it, and in those days nobody wore a helmet, I mean you see a lot of people wearing helmets now but years ago nobody did. Well, I almost stopped in time. The brakes were a lot better than I thought and I didn't hit it, although I fell off and cut my leg a bit. I couldn't believe it. I'd expected much worse.

2

Well, it was the first time I'd tried it and I wasn't very good at it and I wasn't really enjoying it either. It was the last day and I was practising and I saw this, well, I don't know what it was, a sort of depression, there was probably a small stream underneath. Anyway, it sort of went down, and I thought I could just sail across it, you know, through the air and onto the other side but of course I hit the opposite bank and broke my leg, quite badly, because the bindings didn't release as easily as they do now. I felt like a complete idiot. It was so unnecessary.

3

It was deliberate. It wasn't an accident at all. He saw how close I was to scoring and just decided to stop me. And nobody saw it, not even the referee. It really messed my knee up. I was off for the rest of the season.

4

Somehow I knew he wouldn't get over it – it was just too high for him but it was too late to stop him. I knew we would fall. I was just hoping I wouldn't get hurt too badly and I suppose a broken wrist isn't too bad. You have to accept the occasional accident. It's inevitable if you go out a lot. It hasn't put me off.

5

Well, I could feel it going over and knew I couldn't stop it. The thing was, I didn't expect to be rescued. I was hundreds of miles from anywhere in a really remote area and in those temperatures you can't last for more than a couple of hours, even with a life jacket. I had no hope at all. I hate to admit it now but I actually started crying, but obviously no one could hear. It was a miracle someone spotted me.

Test 3

PART 1   Electric Cars

You will hear someone talking about electric cars, past and present. Listen to the recording and for questions 1–10, complete the missing information. You will hear the recording twice.

What kind of cars will we drive in the future? Well, many people believe that the car of the future will be an electric car, powered by a battery. This may sound very revolutionary, but in actual fact electric cars were being manufactured as long ago as 1899 – not many people believe such cars existed then. In that year, a Belgian driver, Camille Jenatzy, broke the land speed record by driving at over 100 kilometres per hour. This was a sensation because at that time no petrol-driven car could manage anything like that speed. To reach such a high speed, Jenatzy made use of a key feature of electric cars, which still exists today. With an electric car, you have a choice. You can design the car to go a very short distance at a high speed or travel a longer distance at a modest speed. The former was what Jenatzy went for.

So electric cars have been around for a long time. They are, of course, much less flexible in their performance than petrol-driven cars but they have one big advantage – there are no exhaust fumes containing dangerous chemicals. Many countries are now introducing legislation to control the harmful emissions from petrol-driven cars and this has led to manufacturers rushing to produce viable electric cars, which don't have these harmful emissions. I'm going to tell you about two of these new electric cars. The first one is called the LA405 and it is being developed in California. It has both an electric unit and a tiny petrol engine. It has a maximum speed of 120 kilometres per hour and can accelerate to 80 kilometres per hour in about 17 seconds. The battery enables the car to travel for about 90 kilometres and then the petrol engine can be used to extend the range by another 140 kilometres. This car even has air-conditioning but this is run through solar panels on the roof, making use of free energy. This solution avoids the problem of draining the battery by making too heavy a demand on it. You can recharge the battery while you are at work because recharge points will be installed in city car parks. Alternatively, you can plug it into the mains at night and it will be ready to drive off in the morning.

Another new electric car is called Impulse, also being developed in California. Like the LA 405, it has two motors, but they are both electric. Its top speed is 160 kilometres per hour and it can accelerate from zero to 95 kilometres in eight seconds, which is a pretty good performance even for a petrol-driven car. Will these cars go into mass production? Only time will tell.

PART 2   A Dissatisfied Customer

You will hear a message left by a customer on a telephone answering machine at the office of Zenith Computer Software Supplies Ltd. Look at the form below and fill in the information for questions 11–20. Listen very carefully as you will hear the recording once only.

Message: Hello. Thank you for calling Zenith Computer Software Supplies Ltd, the firm that can supply you with absolutely anything you require in state-of-the-art computer software. I am afraid that there is no-one in the office at the moment who can deal with your enquiry, but if you leave a message with details of your name, address, contact telephone number and the nature of your enquiry, we will get back to you as soon as possible. Please speak immediately after you hear the tone. Thank you.

John Smith: My name is Dr John Smith and I live at 37 King Street, Marsham, Gloucestershire. You can contact me on this number – four four five, four four six, two nine nine three. I rang you two weeks ago about your Stand Alone Modem, model number FM 2500, which I ordered by telephone and paid for by credit card. According to the invoice, which I have here in front of me, the number is 19292, that was on the thirteenth of January. The salesperson who I dealt with was called Martin Brown and I've got my customer code if that helps – it's 1SM114. You sent me the modem by express courier and I received it the next day, the 14th January. I have no complaints about that – I was delighted to get it so quickly. But when I opened the parcel, the adaptor was not inside. It is a DC ten five V adaptor and I can't use the modem without it – I can't even plug it in. I rang about this last week and spoke to Martin Brown again and he said he would send the adaptor by first class post the same day. He definitely promised that he would. That was more than a week ago and I have still not received it. I need it very urgently indeed because I am setting up an electronic mail network with a number of European universities. Would you please send it immediately? I have been in touch with the manufacturers, but they say I have to get the adaptor through you, as you are the dealers where the modem was purchased, and you hold the guarantee for all relevant parts of the apparatus. It's the adaptor I need and I really can't wait any longer than two more days. I must have it by then or I will face very serious professional difficulties. Please return my call as soon as possible and confirm that you are dealing with this as a matter of urgency.

PART 3   The Uses Of Graphology

You will hear a radio programme in which three people discuss the uses of graphology. For questions 21–30, complete the information using an appropriate word or short phrase. You will hear the recording twice.

Brian Weston: When you apply for a job, how do you expect people to judge your suitability? Will they be looking at your qualifications? Or your previous experience in similar types of jobs? Well, the evidence is that more and more companies, in this country and abroad, are employing graphologists to study people's handwriting. And it's on the basis of their analysis that your psychological suitability for this post will be decided. How fair is this? I talked to two people, Tom Phelps, a practising graphologist and author of 'You and Your Handwriting', and Margot Sawyer, a psychologist at Brimscombe College, who has made a particular study of selection procedures and their effectiveness. So, Tom, what can you tell from looking at someone's handwriting?

Tom Phelps: Well Brian, of course, handwriting reveals deep psychological traits – ambition, sensitivity to other people, how broad-minded you are, all sorts of things like that, but if we're going to talk today mainly about its role in job selection, then I'd also be looking for things that tell me about the applicant's current situation.

Brian Weston: Such as what, exactly?

Tom Phelps: Well, for executive jobs – and this is where graphology is mostly used, in this country anyway – a consultation is quite expensive so you only want to pay that sort of money for these high-level appointments – handwriting can show quite clearly whether or not an applicant is under stress.

Brian Weston: How does it do this?

Tom Phelps: Well, basically, there's going to be quite a lot of variation in the slope, the slant of the writing. The handwriting will be quite erratic. You can also tell if someone is drinking too much, and how they relate to other people and their environment.

Brian Weston: So it's a sort of …

Tom Phelps: It's a pretty effective diagnostic tool, yes, certainly if you judge by the number of companies who are using graphologists in their selection procedures now.

Brian Weston: Right, well all that sounds pretty conclusive to me. But what do you think, Margot?

Margot Sawyer: Yes, that's right, a number of companies are using this technique, but you know, the history of selection is peppered with techniques that don't work very well. I mean, the commonest form of selection is the interview, a one-to-one situation between employer and applicant, and over and over again this has been shown to be a very bad way of selecting people. Virtually all organisations use it, over 90 per cent in fact. So the argument that because firms do something it must be good just doesn't stand up really.

Brian Weston: What are your objections to graphology as such then?

Margot Sawyer: Well, it's the job of psychologists to stand back and to look at techniques objectively, to see if they work empirically. And the research evidence shows overwhelmingly that this technique doesn't come up with what it's meant to. As an example of this, I could point to a typical study. Two graphologists were given samples of handwriting. These were taken from fifty employees in a telecommunications firm who were being assessed for promotion to managerial level within the company. Firstly, the graphologists didn't agree on their results, and secondly, both failed to predict the outcome of the selection procedure.

Brian Weston: So there's no scientific evidence that it actually works?

Tom Phelps: Well, as a graphologist, I could point to at least two studies that show that it does, one conducted in South Africa and another conducted in Israel. And you wouldn't have companies employing the costly services of graphologists year after year if they found what they did to be particularly useless.

Margot Sawyer: Yes, but if you look at the research evidence as a whole, you're obviously going to find one or two studies which actually point favourably to it. I'd have to say that any selection procedure is a bit like looking into a crystal ball. The proof of the success of a technique would be that you had actually identified those people really capable of doing the job. This would constitute empirical proof, and there'd be a very strong case in favour of it.

Tom Phelps: Look, in the US it's been proved that psychologists are strongly opposed to graphologists, for the simple reason that they're afraid they'll take over their jobs. And graphology is being used in therapy too now.

Brian Weston: So are you afraid of being pushed out of a job, Margot?

Margot Sawyer: No, I'm not actually. Psychologists are less interested in graphology than in processes of selection. Firms ask us to come along and look at whether this is working in a particular organisation, and we evaluate the research and come up with a scientifically respectable conclusion.

Brian Weston: And so the debate goes on …

PART 4   The Prizewinners

You will hear five short extracts in which different people comment on their experiences of being prize winners. For questions 31–40, choose the correct option A, B or C. You will hear the recording twice.

1

I went along to the Phoenix theatre and stood on a vast stage and performed for about ten minutes in front of a panel of producers and directors. I'd chosen a speech from 'Romeo and Juliet' … anyway the next day the principal of the stage school called me in and told me I'd won the prize for the Best Drama Student and I thought, 'This is it' and so far it has been. The job offers have just kept pouring in.

2

For me the financial side wasn't what I entered for, although the winner of the Portrait Award does get £5000 in cash. I really just wanted to get some pictures into the exhibition, and the real carrot was the chance of a portrait commission that would go on permanent display in a prestigious art gallery. Winning the award was really just a start for me, and it's only now really that I'm beginning to do what I really want, large scale works in the figurative tradition. I'm simply fascinated by faces.

3

When I entered the competition, I was just seventeen and my horizons were focused on boyfriends and homework. But when I got through the preliminary heats and into the concerto final I felt really happy and relaxed. I just wanted to go out and communicate with the audience. My flute playing really seemed to appeal to them – and to the judges. Even so, I kept to my original plan and went to university to do a degree in English, and I'm glad of those years. I've got an international career as a soloist now but my academic training puts the jetsetting into perspective. You could say I've still got my feet very much on the ground.

4

The competition was held in Switzerland and was open to both boys and girls. For someone from my country where there isn't a strong ballet tradition and there's no national company, it was a chance to assess my talents against the young blood from other countries. I was impressed by the way some people moved, their technique was superb. I made a lot of contacts which were crucial and then as part of the prize I had the chance to give two performances in New York, which got me noticed. It led to the chance for further study and a contract with a leading classical company. Winning the competition was my passport. Without it I'd have gone straight into teaching and there would have been no prospect of a performing career.

5

When I was twelve, I won the under-fourteen cross-country championship and it all came so easily to me, I mean I just put on my trainers and shorts and you couldn't stop me wanting to go faster than anyone else. And I loved circuit training on the track. After the win there was a bit of a reaction and I found it difficult to settle down to school life. People had been telling me I was wonderful and real life seemed a bit of a comedown. I plodded on and eventually got an athletic scholarship to a college on the west coast in the States, and then I realised I was actually good at academic subjects and I went on to study law. I was too successful too young. Life's better now, there's a clearer sense of priorities.

Test 4

You will hear someone describing a traffic accident that he saw. For questions 1–10, complete the notes below, using one or two words. You will hear the recording twice.

Well, I could see the accident extremely clearly indeed from where I was standing, because as I am sure you know, well, you can see for yourself, the hotel overlooks the roundabout. I was looking down on it from my room – it's up on the twentieth floor. I was standing on the balcony just looking down, so you could say I got a bird's eye view. Anyway, this is what I saw – this is how it happened. There was a car approaching the roundabout from the north, and about to enter the roundabout. It was a fast sports car. Actually, there was another car behind it but that wasn't involved in the accident. It was white, the sports car that is. Anyway, there was a van which had already entered the roundabout and was going round it. It was red, probably a Post Office van. And the first car, instead of slowing down or stopping before it entered the roundabout, just drove straight on to it without changing speed at all, and then the van hit the car on the front side and sort of bounced off and then hit it again. This time on the side again, but at the back. However, both vehicles continued moving and left the roundabout by the same exit, straight ahead. I saw it all perfectly clearly. Then just after they had left the roundabout they pulled over and stopped at the side of the road. The car was in front and the van right behind it. And at that point they were both overtaken by a large, very dirty lorry. I mention this because it just missed the car driver as he opened his door and got out. The lorry just drove on and disappeared – I don't think the driver noticed him – there could have been an even worse accident. By this time, the second car – it was a very old, rather slow car, the one I said was behind the sports car to start with – had come along and it stopped too. The car which had been hit was white in colour, by the way. Then all three drivers got out and looked at the damage. Then the third driver, the one who hadn't been involved in the accident, drove off, leaving the other two there. Then what happened next I'm not quite sure about because they were partly hidden by the cars, but there seems to have been some sort of fight and I noticed the sports car drive away – I could still see the van but not the driver, so that's when I got a bit worried and I phoned down to hotel reception to tell them what I'd seen.

You will hear an astronomer talking about the planet Mars. For questions 11–20, complete the table with the missing information. For each answer you will have to write down a number or a word. Listen very carefully as you will hear the recording once only.

Radio Presenter: ... and for today's two-minute science spot, we have Bernard Smith, editor of 'Astronomy Today' who's going to talk to us about the planet Mars, which, as he's going to tell us, is clearly visible in the night sky at the moment.

Bernard Smith: That's right, Anna, you can see it with the naked eye and even with an ordinary pair of binoculars you can get a very good view indeed. Now a lot of people think that Mars is very much like the Earth but that's only true in the sense that the other planets are nothing like Earth. There are many differences between Mars and the Earth. The most obvious difference is that Mars is much smaller, about half the size of the Earth. Whereas Earth has a diameter of 12,714 kilometres, the diameter of Mars is only 6,786 kilometres. One of the consequences of this difference in size is that the force of gravity is much less on Mars. This may sound amazing but you would be able to jump over a fence six metres high on Mars. This is because the force of gravity on Mars is only 38 per cent of what it is on Earth. Another difference is that Mars is much further from the sun than Earth, 141 million miles away compared with 93 million miles in the case of Earth and this means that it receives less than half the sunlight that Earth receives, only 43 per cent of what we get. Because it is further away from the sun, it takes longer to go round it, almost twice as long, so a Martian year lasts 687 Earth days. However, the number of hours in a Martian day is almost the same as the number of hours in a day on Earth. A Martian day is just slightly longer – 24 hours 37 minutes. Another difference is that here on Earth when you look at the night sky you see one moon, whereas on Mars you would see two, both quite small.

As you probably know, it is not possible for human beings to breathe the atmosphere of Mars because it is almost entirely carbon dioxide with only a very tiny amount of oxygen, a mere 0.1 per cent. However, if you were able to stand on the surface of Mars you would notice that some of its physical features, such as valleys and mountains, are much bigger than anything on Earth. Our highest mountain is Mount Everest, which is 8,884 high, but there is a volcano on Mars, it's called Olympus Mons, which is almost three times higher at 24,000 metres.

PART 3   Electronic Books

You will hear a radio programme in which two people, Marcia and Robert, talk about the differences between electronic book discs and conventional printed books. During the interview they express various views. For questions 21–30, indicate which views are expressed by Marcia and which are expressed by Robert, by writing M (for Marcia) or R (for Robert) in the box provided. You may write both initials in one box if both express the same view. You will hear the recording twice.

Radio Presenter: You've probably noticed that you can't buy long-playing records anymore – they've all been replaced by CDs. Is it possible that the same thing could happen to printed books? Will printed books disappear from our lives and be replaced by electronic books? We invited Marcia Brown, a computer expert, and Robert Smith, a novelist, to discuss the issues. You first, Marcia.

Marcia: It is my view that books are the dinosaurs of the 20th century and are about to become extinct. I think that by the second or third decade of the 21st century, books will only be produced in tiny quantities for specialist collectors, if at all. We will obtain all the information we need by inserting CD-ROM discs into handheld computers, or downloading it from the Internet and reading from the screen. In fact, we can do this now. People will prefer this way of reading because of its sheer convenience. For example, the entire Oxford English Dictionary, twenty very heavy volumes in book form, can be placed on a disc that you can carry around in your pocket. The books weigh 66 kilograms. Because discs are so much lighter than books, people will find them much more convenient.

Robert: Well, I think that you are overstating your case quite a bit, Marcia, because although the Oxford English Dictionary can fit onto one disc, it can't be used with a handheld computer. It has to be used with the kind of computer you have on your desk, which certainly can't be carried around. It is much quicker to find the information in a book, to look up a word in a dictionary, for example, than to locate the information on a disc or from the Internet. And even a handheld computer is heavier than a paperback book, although I agree that the actual discs are lighter, but they are useless without something to play them on.

Marcia: Well, I'm not sure I entirely agree. The latest pocket computers are very small and light indeed. Of course, there is a long way to go and a lot of things to improve. We are in the same position as we were with books in the fifteenth century. I think you are forgetting how quickly things catch on and improve. The batteries, for example, although they don't last very long, last a lot longer than they did a few years ago and the image, even in colour, is very clear on the most up-to-date machines. Also, although people like you, Robert, who are used to books and actually like books, can quickly find information in them, people who have grown up using computers from an early age can find the information they need very quickly and often prefer to do it that way. It is very noticeable that young people feel more comfortable with computers than they do with books.

Robert: I can see that certain types of books, especially reference books such as encyclopaedias and dictionaries, are very suitable for using in the form of electronic discs because you can have all the information available in your home or office without lots of space being taken up by large books. But this question of the quality of the image is a very important one. It is possible to call up a street plan on your disc, for example, and find you can't read the street names because they are blurred. Until that is improved, people will still prefer to read print from a page. It's just a much more pleasant experience to hold a book in your hand.

Marcia: I still think you are ignoring the pace of change. Think how fast mobile phones have improved and how popular they have become. When the first printed books appeared more than 500 years ago, I'm sure there were people who thought they were ugly compared with the beautiful, hand-written manuscripts produced by monks. They thought they were losing something valuable and in a sense they were right, but books had the immense advantages of being cheap and practical. It's like that now with books on disc.

Robert: But not cheap, surely. The discs, not to mention the computers themselves, are much more expensive than books. And there are so many different systems, which are not necessarily compatible with each other.

Marcia: It's true that we still have several different formats for disc books – and we need to reach agreement on one format – and that will happen, I'm sure. And prices are still higher than for conventional books but not for long. Quite soon a book in electronic form will be about the same price as a hardback novel. Think of videos – they used to cost much more than books, now they are cheaper. We have to look ahead and imagine how much things will have improved in thirty years' time. That's when there won't be any more bookshops in your town.

Robert: I don't know. What I can see right now is lots of new, very large and impressive bookshops opening up everywhere, which are a pleasure to visit.

Marcia: Yes, because they are facing a lot of competition from computer-based entertainment.

PART 4   Danger And Risk

You will hear five short extracts in which different people talk about danger and risk in their lives.
Task one: for questions 31–35, match the extracts as you hear them with the people, listed A–H.
Task two: for questions 36–40, match the extracts as you hear them with the reasons given by each speaker for taking part in dangerous activities, listed A–H.
Remember that you must complete both tasks as you listen. You will hear the recording twice.

1

Of course, it's nowhere near as dangerous as it looks to the people watching. A lot of it is special effects and there are a lot of things you can't see because they're not in the shot. And everything is well planned in advance to minimise danger. But there is some danger and there are accidents. The main attraction for me is that we're paid very well and don't work very often, although our careers are inevitably short.

2

People think it is dangerous but in fact if you look at the statistics it is much, much safer than driving a car. It's just that jumping out into the air needs more nerve than getting into a car. Once you've jumped out, there's nothing more you can do – you totally rely on your equipment. The sense of exhilaration is marvellous, I just can't get enough of it.

3

I've lived here all my life and I know the area well and if people get into trouble up there I feel that I ought to try and help them. I just can't sit at home watching telly knowing that there's someone up there with a broken leg or something. There's a team of us of course, and if we can't get to the people easily they can bring in the helicopter, but sometimes the weather is so bad that that's not possible. Then we just have to carry people down. It can take hours sometimes.

4

When you go underground, you have to squeeze through some very narrow spaces and that's very difficult mentally. Sometimes you think that you are going to be stuck, you feel trapped and you start to panic. Sometimes it happens that people completely freak out – and then it is really bad. It's the confined space, you see, some people just can't handle it. But what I like is feeling the panic, sometimes letting it almost take over, and then overcoming it and carrying on.

5

Well, for me it's a job and although it's not particularly well-paid, it's not boring and predictable like a lot of other jobs. You don't know from one day to the next what you will be doing. There's a lot of different things going on and you need to have a lot of different skills. When you hear the bell and jump into the appliance, and race through the streets, you never know what you're going to find when you arrive. Could be really dangerous, could be a simple job, you just don't know.

Test 5

You will hear someone talking about the development of the telephone. For questions 1–10, fill in the missing information. You will hear the recording twice.

Presenter: Welcome everybody to our monthly meeting. I know you've all been looking forward to the chance to hear tonight's guest speaker, Tom Wilkinson, who's going to talk to us about the history of telephones. So without more ado, Tom Wilkinson.

Tom Wilkinson: Good evening, ladies and gentlemen. It gives me great pleasure to be here tonight to talk about a subject that has fascinated me for many years, the telephone and how it works.

These days, when you dial a friend in Australia, it's easy to take the whole thing for granted. After a few clicks and whirrs, you're through. Thousands of miles vanish in an instant. It's so easy. But anyone over 50 will remember a time when it could take hours to phone a friend just a few hundred miles away. In fact, if we take a brief look at the development of the phone system, we'll find that not much changed at all between 1880 and 1950.

In 1880, when the first brass and mahogany phone arrived, it cost £45, the equivalent of a year's wages for the average working man. In those far off days, the airwaves were virtually silent. There were no exchanges in Britain and most of the telephones in use were installed in large country houses so the wealthy could talk to their servants and each other.

By the 1920's, there were manual exchanges in towns and cities up and down the country, the cost of telephones had come down considerably and far more of us were installing the new wonder instrument. But by 1930, there were still only a few experimental automatic exchanges. This meant that all calls had to go through an operator. When you picked up the receiver the operator was automatically alerted at the exchange: basically a little flap dropped on her switchboard or a light came on and she knew you wanted to use the phone. With the Magneto telephone, the only alternative to the standard model, you cranked a handle on the side of the phone to alert the operator who then rang you to ask what number you wanted.

The system then, and it lasted into the 1970s in some areas, was that the operator would decide how to route your call. She would contact the next exchange on your route and the operator at that exchange would either connect you or hand you on to what could turn out to be the first in a whole series of operators, depending on how far your call had to go. And if one of the exchanges on the way happened to be engaged, you simply had to wait until it cleared. Incredibly, the last manual exchange was still operating in Abingdon, Oxfordshire, as late as 1975. People in the area still had phones without dials and all their calls had to be put through, manually, by the operator.

How things have changed! Today a lightning-fast, digital system works out how to route your call in a split second, and a call from London to Oxford may go via Edinburgh if all the more direct routes are engaged. Such is the speed of modern technology that we notice no delay.

In an emergency, the old system was horribly slow and not always reliable. But there was something rather grand about the stately progress of a call that could only be achieved through the skills of a series of individual operators devoting their energies to keeping you in touch.

You will hear an answerphone message announcing details of rail and steam attractions at the weekend. For questions 11–20, complete the information sheet according to the information you hear. Listen very carefully as you will hear the recording once only.

Thank you for calling the special information line with details of special Rail and Steam attractions this August weekend. We've got three attractions to tell you about, at Swanley, Fairbourne and Matlock.

Attraction number one is the Central Railway at Swanley. Step back in time on this steam railway that will take you on an hour's trip through unspoilt countryside. Especially recommended for children over five who will enjoy the chance, after the train ride, to visit the engine sheds and see the old steam trains collected here from different parts of the country.

How did telegraph systems work? Here's your opportunity to find out in the working re-creation of a telegraph office where visitors can operate the equipment, and there's a post office where the kids can help sort the parcels as they come off the train in the delivery area. Sundays only, ten to six, adults £5, children £2.50.

The second attraction is the Fairbourne Connection, a narrow-gauge railway that runs for ten miles along the seashore, passing through stations over a hundred years old, two of which have recently been restored to their former glory. Many visitors are tempted to take the short ferry connection across the bay to Henderson Island where they can visit a village built in Italian style. There's an open-air restaurant and gardens to enjoy. One train only per day at 10.45 from Fairbourne station. Adults £7.50, children free.

What do you know about trams? Our third suggestion for steam enthusiasts is a trip to a Tramway Museum at Matlock where there's a collection of restored horse-drawn, steam and electric trams. All rides are free once you've paid the entrance fee, and you can have as many rides as you like. This weekend is a special teddy bear weekend and any child bringing an adult and a teddy will be allowed in free. The route covers a one-mile scenic track, and if the weather's not up to much, there are models to play with and a video to watch on the history of the tram. Entrance fee £6.50 per adult, £2 for accompanying children.

PART 3

You will hear a radio interview with a person who is blind. For questions 21–28, choose the most suitable answers (A, B, C or D). You will hear the recording twice.

Jenny White: In the third of my occasional series, 'How do they do it?' I talked to James Powell, who's been blind since the age of three, about how he views the world. I asked him first about how his blindness came about.

James: Actually, I suffered from a rare condition, but at least it's a well-understood phenomenon. It's a tumour which attacks the retina. Even when the tumour is removed, it can lead to further complications, but if you survive into your teens, you're more or less safe.

Jenny White: So do you have any vision at all?

James: No, I don't see at all. Some people, even people who are totally blind, retain some kind of visual concept, but I really have none. The understanding I have of the visual world has mostly been acquired through listening to other people and learning about how they live. Basically, I am in a world where there is no light, no colour and no shape.

Jenny White: So how does this affect you?

James: I suppose one of the main problems about being blind is getting out of yourself and getting across to other people. And even if you are a person with lots of ideas and you know how to conduct a conversation and so on, you can miss the fact that the person you're talking to looks awful because they've got flu, or has a wonderful suntan and have obviously been somewhere terrific – so

you don't think of saying: 'Gosh, where have you been?' That's the difficulty about being blind.

People also imagine that if you can't see, you can't hear and can't think. There is some truth in this, because so much of hearing actually depends on the organisation of sight. It isn't true that blind people have got very sharp ears and always know what's going on; in fact, sight is the central organising sense, and so not being able to see makes it difficult to use your ears as intelligently as you would like. Consequently, blind people may find it difficult to tell what is going on when there are a large number of people in a place.

Jenny White: Yes, I can appreciate that.

James: And, you know, if you're the sort of person who as a matter of course knocks over tables laden with china or causes similar physical calamities, you must learn to take it without letting it knock you off balance. I think that if I can learn how to keep calm, other people will take their lead from me: a show of anxiety or panic doesn't help people to conquer their fear of blind people.

Jenny White: Right. Tell me about your schooldays. How did you relate to people then?

James: I was totally segregated when I was at school, which was something I find very hard to forgive. It was extremely damaging. One of the arguments for it is you concentrate resources by segregating handicapped children, but I don't think anything can outweigh the social disadvantages and the intellectual isolation which come about as a result of segregation. I found it really difficult to adjust to living in the real world and mixing with ordinary people.

Jenny White: Do you think things have improved now for people in a similar condition to yours?

James: Yes, I think things are changing for the better – all around me I see blind people who are working hard at finding a better life for themselves. The most important change since I was at school is that there is now a strong move towards the integration of blind children in mainstream education. As social integration grows, sighted people are exposed much more to blind people, and I think that's breaking down prejudice.

Jenny White: You've got a responsible job. Is that a source of pride?

James: Yes, I suppose it is – I enjoy teaching very much and I've always been interested in computers. I was a computer programmer for a long time, and having had previous teaching experience, I've got the pedagogic tradition, so I know how to put a course together. And, importantly, I give classes to sighted as well as to non-sighted students.

Jenny White: And what are your plans for the future?

James: Well, at the moment I'm trying to write a book – it's something I do in my spare time. In a sense, the last thing I want to do is write about being blind, because that would be the least integrative thing I could do, but I find that I can't really turn my mind to the other things until I find some way of answering the basic questions about blindness, and there are a lot of them. In some ways, as I get older, although I'm technically more capable, blindness becomes more difficult to cope with. It may well be that writing a book, as for so many other people, will be a therapeutic experience.

PART 4 Performing In Public

You will hear five short extracts in which different people talk about performing in public.
Task one: for questions 29–33, match the extracts as you hear them with the people, listed A–H.
Task two: for questions 34–38, match the extracts as you hear them with the actions, listed A–H.
Remember that you must complete both tasks as you listen. You will hear the recording twice.

1

The physical effect of nerves on the body can be absolutely shattering for those who perform in public. Why should this be so? Well, if you've always been under pressure, and you've never admitted it, you've just gone on looking and sounding good, then one day the nervous system can just collapse. It just says I can't take it any more. The fear of letting people down becomes too much.

2

I had actually played this particular concerto many, many times before, but on this particular occasion, I really don't know why it was such a nerve-racking experience. We'd had the usual rehearsals with the orchestra and they'd gone really well. So, on the night, I arrived, bowed, sat down, it came to my turn to perform, I looked at the keyboard. And I was just gripped by terror. I found that my knees were knocking, my neck ached, I couldn't see properly, it was as if I wasn't there. I just didn't know what I was supposed to be doing.

3

I think it's a bit different for me and for some other people. I mean, if you're a trumpet player, or a singer or an actor, then you have to do it to script. When you're speaking, as I have to do when I'm defending someone in court, or if I've been asked to speak at a conference, you know all the points you want to put forward but you can do them in any order you like. However with playing you've actually got to do it when it says you've got to do it and that's what causes the nerves, you see your bit coming up, and you think, oh no, I can never do this.

4

My cue is getting nearer, I'm not going to be able to go on, I know I'm not going to be able to go on. I'm stuck here. My shoes have been stuck to the floor. Doesn't anybody understand this? I'm all alone. No one can help me. I'm going to walk out into that spotlight and everyone is going to know. How can this happen to me, after all these years? And the others, my fellow players. They must keep their side of the bargain. They mustn't look at me, they mustn't look me in the eyes or I'm done for.

5

I wasn't playing the trumpet at the time, I think I was filling in on side drums and I took these tranquillisers, not many, and I found myself very relaxed, very relaxed indeed, in fact too relaxed, and I remember well when we were playing in the concert. I should have been playing the side-drum going *bom bu bu bom*, something like that and instead of that I was going *bu bu bu bom* and I was happily banging away doing this and the conductor looked across at me and he was looking at me very strangely, emphasising his beat, looking very hard at me and I thought, 'He wants me to play louder', and being very relaxed about it on these tranquillisers I started to play louder and louder and of course it was all wrong, he was trying to tell me, you know, get it right.